Mindfulness Workbook
for Perfectionism

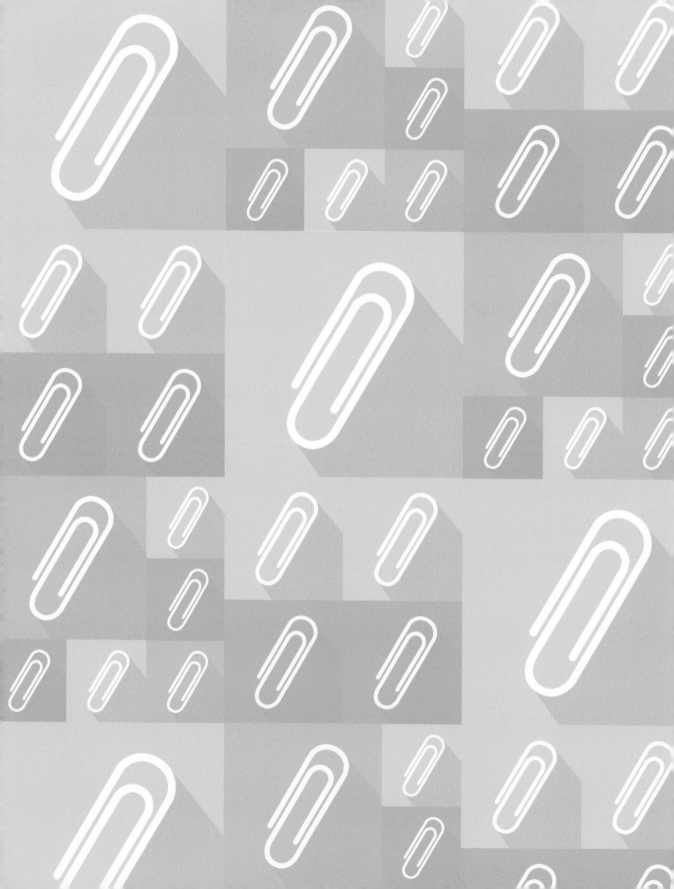

Mindfulness Workbook for Perfectionism

Effective Strategies to Overcome
Your Inner Critic and Find Balance

Elaine A. Thomas, PSYD

ROCKRIDGE
PRESS

First Rockridge Press trade paperback edition 2022

For general information on our other products and services, please contact our Customer Care Department within the United States at (866) 744-2665, or outside the United States at (510) 253-0500.

Paperback ISBN: 978-1-63878-449-4 | eBook ISBN: 978-1-63878-655-9

Manufactured in the United States of America

Interior and Cover Designer: Tricia Jang
Art Producer: Sue Bischofberger
Editor: Katherine De Chant
Production Manager: Martin Worthington

Illustration used under license from shutterstock.com.

10 9 8 7 6 5 4 3 2 1 0

To the courageous,
perfectly imperfect souls
who take steps to
transform suffering.

CONTENTS

INTRODUCTION viii

HOW TO USE THIS BOOK x

PART I

AN OVERVIEW OF PERFECTIONISM AND MINDFULNESS....................1

1 Understanding Perfectionism....................................3

2 Introduction to Mindfulness..................................17

PART II

PRACTICING MINDFULNESS TO OVERCOME PERFECTIONISM.............31

3 Beginner's Mind: Embracing a New Perspective....................33

4 Nonjudgment: Stepping Back from Your Inner Critic............................47

5 Acceptance: Acknowledging What Is,
Not Clinging to What Should Be..................................61

6 Patience: Not Rushing Yourself.................................79

7 Trust: Choosing Self-Compassion over Self-Doubt..............................95

8 Non-Striving: Seeing Yourself as a Process, Not a Product...................109

9 Letting Go: Making Peace with What You Can't Control......................127

MOVING FORWARD WITH MINDFULNESS 139

RESOURCES 142

REFERENCES 145

INDEX 149

INTRODUCTION

As a practicing psychologist for more than two decades, I have repeatedly encountered the harmful effects of unbridled perfectionism in my patients and their family members. "Perfectionist" is also a label that I would apply to myself–I'm no stranger to the patterns of thoughts, behaviors, and feelings associated with perfectionism and how they can cloud what is really important, erode well-being, and interfere with mental health. In my work, where I aim to stay informed about cutting-edge knowledge and treatment approaches, I now know that perfectionism is a shared feature of many different mental health conditions. There is now a considerable body of research dedicated to perfectionism, and it is widely understood that addressing perfectionism directly can result in a positive outcome, while not doing so can be a barrier to significant change.

Researchers have made tremendous strides in identifying what perfectionism is, studying how it interferes with people's lives, and determining that its treatment is essential, but there isn't yet a consensus on *how* to treat it. While cognitive behavioral therapy (CBT) for perfectionism is the most studied approach and is effective, there is no one way to treat any psychological difficulty. There must be convincing evidence that the method is likely to work, but your confidence and preference for a particular method are as essential as the method. Many studies have revealed the benefit of mindfulness approaches in treating mental health conditions in which perfectionism appears. Mindfulness helps you recognize that your perfectionism doesn't serve you. It also gives you the motivation to change it, the courage to try new things, and the inner wisdom to discern what is helpful to you and what is not.

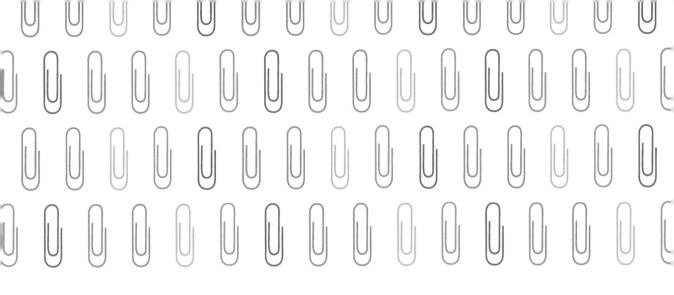

In developing the exercises and practices for this workbook, I've drawn on techniques and tools that have been proven effective for conditions similar to perfectionism. Some of them come from well-established treatments that I discuss in the next chapter. Others come from well-researched methods to enhance the quality of your life. Included in each chapter is a method for you to track how the exercises and practices may be helping you. But while I offer evidence-based tools, this book is not a substitute for professional help in any form. It is no substitute for medication that has been prescribed to you, or any other course of treatment recommended by a mental health professional.

Perfectionism is also associated with several mental health conditions. If you have anxiety, depression, an eating disorder, or problems in interpersonal relationships, it will be vital for you to seek help for these conditions. Unfortunately, there can be stigma associated with seeking help from a mental health professional, so you may experience feelings of shame or think something is wrong with you. But you don't need to feel that way. Mental health, like physical health, ebbs and flows and can sometimes manifest as chronic difficulties in functioning or in your well-being. Know that you don't have to struggle alone. I've included a list of resources at the end of this book to help you find assistance from the many experts who have devoted their professional lives to understanding how to help you.

This workbook is a way for you to understand more about perfectionism and explore new skills to address it. It may also be used as a tool in your treatment and may have been recommended by your mental health professional.

HOW TO USE THIS BOOK

The workbook is organized into nine chapters. The first two chapters describe perfectionism and mindfulness, respectively, so it will be more helpful to read these before completing the remaining chapters. The subsequent chapters are organized around the seven pillars of mindfulness and describe how each of these pillars relates to perfectionism. In these chapters, you will find mindfulness practices, reflection exercises, and other tools. Try each practice several times before deciding whether it may be helpful to you. Give each one your good-faith effort and remember that they are called practices because they are skills that benefit from repetition, and each chapter builds on the preceding chapters. Make sure to also have realistic expectations—some things may seem immediately helpful, some may be useful after practice, and others may not make it into your toolbox of strategies. Take your time going through each chapter. Complete no more than one new exercise and practice each day. Above all, let go of any expectation that there is a right way to complete the workbook.

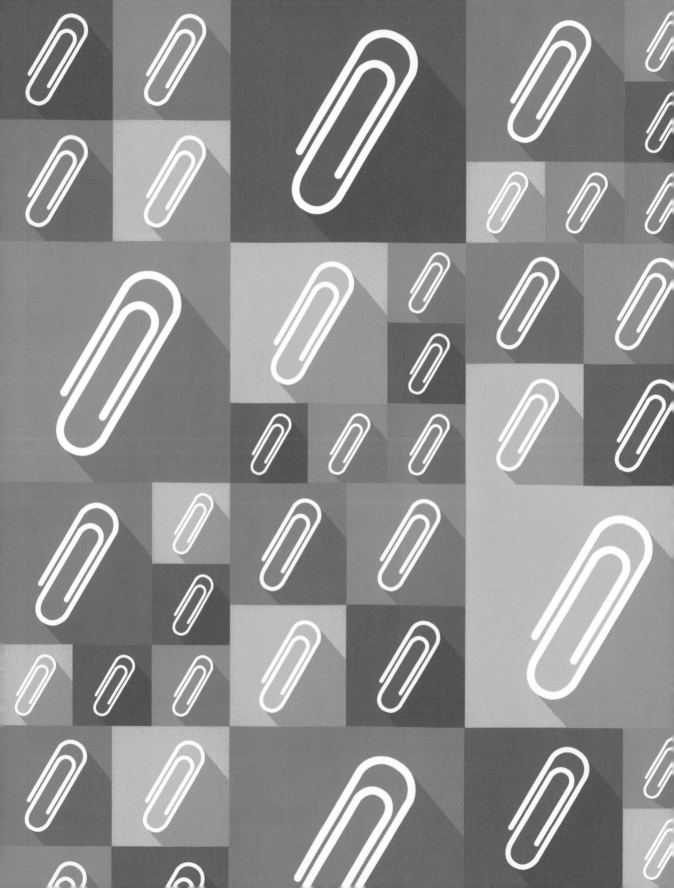

PART I

An Overview of Perfectionism and Mindfulness

The first section of this book explores perfectionism and mindfulness as individual concepts. This will give you a basis for the exercises and practices and help you build a new understanding of how perfectionism impacts your life and how understanding it through the lens of mindfulness can assist you.

The perfectionism chapter describes the many ways perfectionism is expressed, the common ways it develops, the positive and negative aspects of perfectionism, and the cycles that sustain problematic perfectionism. The mindfulness chapter provides a clear description that separates the hype from reality, emphasizes what it is and what it is not, and explains how the major principles of mindfulness may be helpful to those who are perfectionistic.

Throughout the book, you'll find examples of people that illustrate particular points, but the case studies do not reflect the lives of real people. Although they are based on scenarios of living, breathing individuals, they do not describe actual persons.

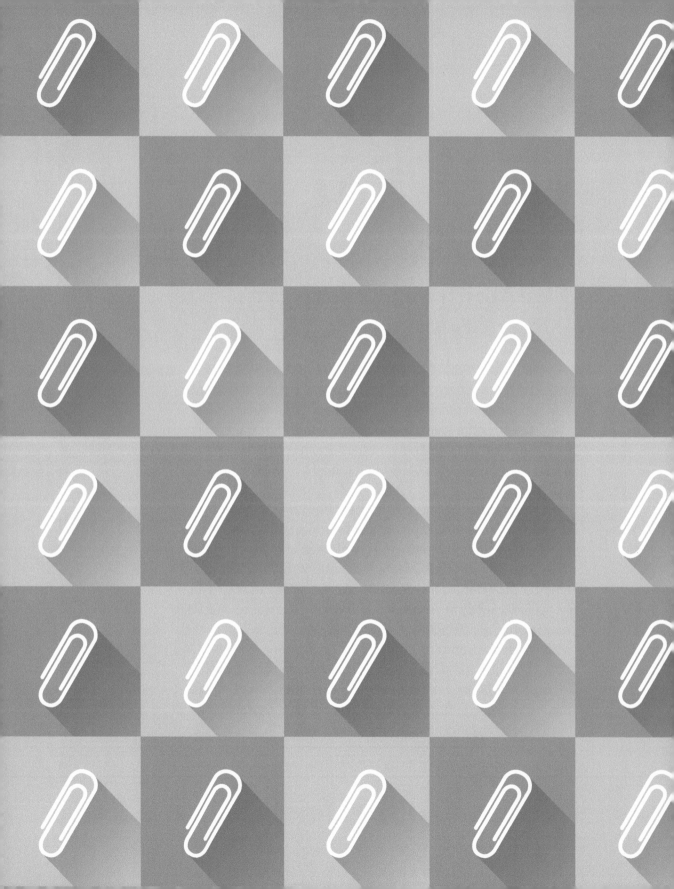

Understanding Perfectionism

Perfectionism, like any other human characteristic, will present itself distinctively and uniquely in an individual. But the patterns of perfectionism are similar across individuals and have been observed in scientific studies and by clinicians. It might be a relief to see your experiences reflected in the patterns described here because it helps you know that you're not alone. By identifying your patterns, you're also likely to better understand your perfectionism and how it serves or doesn't serve you.

Perfectionism has numerous facets. For many, it is a gem in the rough. The rugged and rough parts hide the parts that can be exposed to permit the brilliance to shine. This workbook aims to help you understand and round out the rough, rugged parts that apply to you so that you can embrace the brilliance.

When I use the term "perfectionism" in this book, I refer to the facets of perfectionism that cause difficulties for you. In this chapter, we'll explore different facets of perfectionism, how perfectionism manifests, its origins, positive aspects of perfectionism, and how perfectionism perpetuates distress and suffering.

TAI BREAKS DOWN

Tai took great pride in exceeding performance targets as a sales rep for a pharmaceutical firm. She flourished in response to the accolades from her boss and proudly displayed the trophies she had received for state and regional awards. Known as the "best dressed" in social and work circles, she also made a great effort to exercise five times a week, eat healthy meals, and maintain her trim size-four figure. But while the high-performance accolades she had received all her life had motivated her to excel, after receiving a national award, she began sleeping fretfully at night. Tai started every day in a panic, wondering if she would make the daily target she had set for herself. At times she found that she wasn't listening to customers, and she left meetings ruminating about what she could have done better and berating herself. Although already accustomed to working forty to sixty hours a week since college, she began to put more effort into preparing for meetings by researching the individual she was meeting and making sure she was meticulously put-together. One Saturday morning, she cried uncontrollably after explaining to her best friend, again, why she couldn't go for coffee and had to work because she had missed a sale. Feeling overwhelmed, sad, anxious about her future, and exhausted, Tai began to think that something was wrong with her and questioned her very existence.

What Is Perfectionism?

Perfectionism is a multifaceted personality characteristic. A core feature is rigidly holding excessively high standards tied to your self-worth. If these standards are not met, self-criticism, distress, suffering, and other negative consequences persist.

Perfectionism is not always problematic. There are many ways in which perfectionism maintains excellence and motivates achievement, creativity, and productivity. It becomes problematic when the distress at not meeting standards becomes frequent and severe, and over time begins to affect your self-concept or results in self-defeating behaviors. Any of the emotions we experience as humans could occur in response to not meeting standards. Typically, these are sadness, anxiety, shame, hopelessness, or anger. Thoughts resulting from not meeting standards can include self-blame, criticism, overestimating the significance, and worst-case scenario predictions. Self-defeating behaviors can include overworking, excessive checking, procrastinating, and avoidance.

For some, perfectionism can be most prominent in one or two life domains. Some people may be especially perfectionistic in work performance and physical appearance, like Tai. Others may be perfectionistic across many life domains, such as in work, school, how they look (clothing, weight, exercise, diet), relationships, or décor. Perfectionism may appear in any area of your life that is important to you.

Perfectionism is a risk factor for several mental health conditions, including anxiety, depression, obsessive-compulsive disorder, eating disorders, and problems interacting with others.

Perfectionism is also a process that, if left unaddressed, can perpetuate these disorders. Although the examples I've provided may include those who suffer from these mental health conditions, this book does not address the perfectionism associated with these specific conditions. Instead, it gives a general description of perfectionism and how it manifests. As mentioned previously, this book is no substitute for mental health treatment—it's important to seek treatment if you suffer from one of these mental health conditions.

The Difference between Perfectionism and the Pursuit of Excellence

Perfectionism and pursuit of excellence both involve aiming high. They share aspiring for extraordinary achievements and setting goals outside of what is average. The difference is that perfectionism demands exceptional performance. The pursuit of excellence, on the other hand, aims for exceptional performance while acknowledging that it isn't always achievable.

Perfectionism results in negative, self-defeating consequences when standards and goals are not met. In contrast, the pursuit of excellence does not negatively affect the person when the goals are not achieved. Instead, people who pursue excellence incorporate new learning to help them grow. Perfectionism focuses on the outcome, whereas the pursuit of excellence focuses on both the process and the outcome. In perfectionism, the person doesn't only aspire to excellence—they aspire to perfection. Excellence is not good enough.

A key difference is the way you respond to failure and mistakes. Pursuing goals and high standards in perfectionism is often associated with negative emotions such as anxiety and fear, while pursuing excellence is not. In perfectionism, the evaluation of worth as a person depends exclusively on the pursuit and achievement of standards and goals. Those who pursue excellence do not depend on achieving difficult goals to validate their self-esteem and self-worth. They obtain a sense of worthiness and effectiveness from accomplishments and other things.

Perfectionists have very low levels of self-acceptance, whereas those who strive for excellence have high levels of self-acceptance. Perfectionists are often persistently very unhappy and dissatisfied with themselves and their lives because they consistently feel they're not meeting the standards they set for themselves. In pursuit of excellence without perfectionism, people do not consistently feel they are falling short of their standards and are typically satisfied overall with themselves and their lives.

The Roots of Perfectionism

There are multiple pathways to perfectionism, and yours will not be quite the same as someone else's. Perfectionism is the outcome of a combination of factors occurring across your life. More important, it persists and causes difficulties because of certain ways of thinking, behaving, and feeling.

At the highest level, as is true for most human characteristics, perfectionism is a joint product of your biological makeup and your experiences. Although the relative contribution of each is impossible to determine, experiences are likely the major contributor. This is good news, as we can do little to change our biological makeup, but we can do much to change our experiences. We control how we decide what is important, how we make meaning of our experiences, what we choose to prioritize, and how we respond to our thoughts and feelings. Some of these experiences that are potent contributors are external to us and occur in our environment; other experiences arise internally within the parameters of our thoughts and feelings. Early childhood experiences in multiple contexts–such as family, school, friends, and other communities–also shape how we see ourselves or our self-concept. Perfectionists have usually had experiences that result in beliefs that high standards are essential and that their self-worth is dependent on achieving and maintaining these standards.

Parental Expectations and Modeling

Children with parents who set high expectations and tend to praise and reward these achievements exclusively are prone to developing perfectionism. Parents who set these high, often unrealistic, standards also tend to be critical when these standards are not met. Children of these parents experience pressure to conform to expectations and pursue high standards because they have been rewarded when they achieve them. Their self-worth then becomes closely associated with high achievement, solidifying their beliefs about performance. Parental response to mistakes can also be a contributing factor. If parents respond with disappointment, negative emotion, or criticism, this too contributes to persisting beliefs about never making mistakes. Since children also learn by observing others, they may watch perfectionistic parents who demonstrate these patterns and emulate them.

Cultural or Societal Expectations

In some cultures, there is a pressure to conform. Although much of this comes directly from parents and family, the pressures are often similar among families with a shared national origin, ethnicity, or religious background. They may involve any area of life and can include rules for appearance, behavior, etc. For example, some parents expect high educational achievement for their children, which the child then internalizes as a way for them to increase connectedness and belonging. Some people with marginalized status make great efforts to counter negative stereotypes others may have of them, which may be expressed in perfectionism.

Fear of Inadequacy and Unlovability

Fear that we are inadequate or unlovable often drives us to compulsively strive to meet high standards that would serve as external validation of worthiness and lovability. Deep down, you may feel inadequate, have low self-worth, and feel unlovable and defective, so you work hard at perfection to prove to yourself that you are not these things. Childhood experiences of harsh and demanding parents, bullying and cruelty at the hands of peers, and perceptions that others don't value your differences all contribute to this perception of self. These experiences heighten your concern about how others see and accept you, and you work hard at perfection so that others may accept, like, and care about you.

Desire to Feel in Control

Perfectionism often occurs in tandem with anxiety. People with high anxiety levels tend to have pessimistic predictions and expectations of the future. To try to prevent these pessimistic predictions from happening, they often focus on attempting to control the future and having fixed ideas of what the future ought to bring.

Types of Perfectionism

Scholars and researchers describe perfectionism as being multidimensional. This means that perfectionism has many components or facets, and each facet may be present in an individual to a different degree or not at all. Another way to think of it is as if perfectionism were a cake with many layers. Each layer is a different flavor and has a particular thickness. In one cake, there may be just two or three thick layers, while in another cake, there may be several layers—some very thin, others very thick.

Researchers have used many different models to study and describe perfectionism. Drs. Paul Hewitt, Gordon Flett, and Samuel Mikail created the Comprehensive Model of Perfectionistic Behavior (CMPB) that describes three different facets of perfectionism. One facet is how perfectionism presents in your thinking. Perfectionists often engage in repetitive thinking, reminding themselves of the importance of their goals as well as criticizing themselves and their performance. Another facet is perfectionists' investment in how they appear to others. Perfectionists spend much effort actively promoting their perfection, avoiding displaying their imperfection, and not disclosing their flaws to others. Drs. Hewitt and Flett are also the authors of one of the most widely used measures of perfectionism, the Multidimensional Perfectionism Scale, which captures the last personality facet of perfectionism. This scale measures three distinct but related forms of perfectionism: self-oriented perfectionism, other-oriented perfectionism, and socially prescribed perfectionism.

Self-Oriented Perfectionism

In self-oriented perfectionism, the person believes that setting and meeting exceedingly high standards is essential. They strive to be perfect, expect to be perfect, and hold being perfect as critical to their existence, even though the standards are often unrealistic and unachievable. When those manifesting self-oriented perfectionism do not achieve the exceedingly high standards they set for themselves, they become self-critical. Most important, they use the achievement of standards as an indicator of their self-worth.

Other-Oriented Perfectionism

In other-oriented perfectionism, the person expects that others should and will conform to exceedingly high standards. The expectation is that others will strive to be perfect and achieve perfection. When others do not fulfill these high standards, the person becomes critical, blaming, and rejecting. In this form of perfectionism, individuals are critical of others, whereas they are critical of themselves in the other forms.

Socially Prescribed Perfectionism

In socially prescribed perfectionism, the person believes that others expect them to achieve exceedingly high standards and require them to be perfect. They think that others will be highly critical of them if they fail to meet standards and expectations, so they feel pressure to meet expectations and conform to secure others' approval.

Common Perfectionist Characteristics

Perfectionism manifests itself differently in each person. This is true partly because each person has, among other things, a unique set of life experiences, current circumstances, goals, and necessities. It is also true because perfectionism is a complex personality characteristic that comes in many forms. You may have already recognized yourself in one of the three forms of perfectionism described—having unrelenting standards for yourself, expecting others to behave in ways consistent with exceedingly high standards, or believing that others expect you to conform to perfection. There are also other common characteristics among perfectionists. The following descriptions do not include all aspects of perfectionism, but some of them will likely resonate with you.

Harshly Critical

Perfectionists tend to offer severe judgments of themselves and others when perfection is not achieved. There is no flexibility in perfection as an outcome. When the desired result doesn't happen, perfectionists will often cruelly engage in internal self-talk deriding themselves and their performance. Making a mistake is often cause for more intense self-criticism. Two binaries form the basis for self-judgment—perfect or worthless, excellent or terrible. Judging yourself in this way results in feelings of disappointment, inadequacy, and unhappiness, while judging other people internally and out loud often results in strained and distant relationships.

Unreasonable Standards

The standards of perfectionists are rigid and extreme. These standards also become central to life and are associated with a compulsive need to attain them. Since achieving these exceedingly high standards 100 percent of the time is impossible, the perfectionist is often left disappointed. Simply put, perfection as a standard is unachievable. For many, setting exceedingly high standards is an attempt to avoid criticism and failure. It often comes with excessive preparation, leaving the person exhausted and with little room for relaxation, recreation, pleasure, and satisfaction. Evidence of excessive standards includes inflexible rules, "shoulds" and "musts," attention to detail, and preoccupation with time and efficiency.

Low Self-Worth

Self-worth is based on the achievement of perfection. Perfectionists evaluate themselves narrowly–they are valuable only to the extent to which they achieve their standards. They often feel inadequate and inferior to others, letting their worry about self and identity take center stage. Feelings of shame–a sense that something is fundamentally wrong with the self–are common. Many perfectionists are aware of these feelings of inadequacy and defectiveness. Others may not be consciously aware of the role that striving for perfection plays in developing feelings of unworthiness.

Motivated by Fear

Many perfectionists are motivated by a fear of failure. Working for and aiming for very high standards is a way to avoid failure and the negative feelings that come with facing it. For many perfectionists, failure, mistakes, and errors are to be avoided at all costs because those things come with feelings of shame, disappointment, and embarrassment. Perfectionists interpret failure as evidence that they are inadequate and unworthy. For those who believe that others expect them to be perfect, fear of failure drives perfectionism to prevent people from being angry, losing interest, or abandoning them.

Perfectionistic Thinking

Perfectionists often engage in worry and rumination. These are both types of repetitive thinking that are associated with unpleasant feelings. Worry involves repeatedly thinking about something happening in the future for which there is no clear outcome. Perfectionists often worry about whether they will achieve their goals, making mistakes, their performance, and how someone is judging them. Rumination involves repetitive thinking about the self and the past. Perfectionists often ruminate about how they are preparing, their need to be perfect, not living up to expectations, how they might have achieved a better performance in the past, how they could meet their ideal self-image in the future, their negative judgments of themselves, and their judgments of other people. Perfectionists also tend to be very rigid in defining their standards for themselves and how to achieve them: "I should, I must, I ought to . . ." Other patterns in thinking include attending selectively to a small detail, interpreting the significance of an event to be much larger than it is, and seeing things in all-or-nothing ways.

How Perfectionism Shows Up in Your Life

Perfectionism may present in different areas of your life. It may be helpful to consider different life domains and take an account of the ways it shows up and causes difficulties for you. You might be more aware of how perfectionism appears in one domain and less aware of how much it affects another. It's important to remember that when you decide to shift your perfectionism, it is not productive or realistic to make multiple changes at once. It is most helpful to make small changes, and one way to do so is to start with understanding yourself and shifting things in one life domain at a time. Start with the area that might have lower instances of perfectionism to maximize your chances of success.

Academics and School

Perfectionists prioritize achievement. For younger children in school, it means perpetually striving for straight As and perfect scores on tests and quizzes. As students get older, they work for high class rankings and enter competitive programs. As college or university approaches, they fixate on high scores on standardized tests, entrance to very competitive schools, comparison to peers, and packing a schedule to demonstrate high achievement status. The term "overachiever" is often used to describe these patterns. But the fear that you won't achieve a perfect performance can result in procrastination and a pattern of scrambling at the last minute to complete tasks, avoiding challenging tasks, or generally underachieving. Schooling often ingrains the idea that your self-worth equates to your achievement, leading to unhappiness and a lack of balance in life.

Parenting

Perfectionist parents are often anxious about the quality of their parenting and become invested in a particular way of parenting. They usually take more blame than is realistic for their children's mistakes, have very clear ideas of how they want their children to behave and evolve into independent persons, and are overinvolved in their children's lives. Sometimes parents repeat the patterns of their own parents and are harsh, critical, and authoritarian.

Professional Life

Perfectionists are often workaholics. They work long hours and extend themselves to do whatever it takes to achieve performance goals. Because of this overcommitment they drive themselves and others to produce, and are often highly prized employees.

As bosses, perfectionists may micromanage and be critical of others who do not share their willingness to work longer and harder than most. It can be uncomfortable for the employees they manage to work for such a critical and demanding person. On the other hand, perfectionists are often high achievers who are well-suited for professions and occupations that require years of school and primarily individual work.

Health and Fitness

Specific, often obsessive, requirements for diet, exercise, and physical appearance are common among perfectionists, as is the pursuit of the thin ideal portrayed in popular media. They may focus on adhering to specific regimens for eating and training and criticize themselves for deviating from these regimens. These exceptional standards may even shift into problematic eating patterns and qualify as an eating disorder. Many perfectionists become athletes, bringing their desire for superior performance to training and competition and dedicating many hours to conditioning and practice. In sports, perfectionists find a home where their requirements meet the requirements of coaches and spectators who welcome and reward their efforts and success.

Romantic Relationships

Romantic relationships can be complicated when you expect perfection in the other person and in your connection with them. Romantic partners may find it challenging to live up to expectations, and the perfectionist is often disappointed. Some perfectionists may put a lot of energy into meeting very high standards for themselves and then suffer disappointment when they don't meet these standards or when the other person does not provide adequate reassurance. It may leave them feeling abandoned, rejected, misunderstood, and preoccupied with how the other person feels. By setting unrealistic standards for a partner, some perfectionists may abandon the hope of a romantic relationship.

Social Life

Perfectionists often struggle in social relationships. Those who believe that others expect them to be perfect are often lonely and feel disconnected from others because they assume those people are constantly judging and evaluating them. Feeling pressure to live up to others' expectations can also cause perfectionists to try to present an image of flawlessness, competence, and control and to hide imperfections—even though this unrealistic façade isn't conducive to authentic relationships. Other perfectionists may struggle with repeated disappointments because others do not live up to their expectations, making it difficult to develop genuine connections.

Public Image

Many perfectionists put a lot of effort into their public image, making sure that others see a flawless, perfect version of themselves. There are three facets of this self-presentation: curating and presenting an ideal image, keeping guard to avoid slipping up and showing the imperfection, and never discussing mistakes or flaws with others. As a result of a focus on this persona, the true self of the perfectionist gets lost. Perfectionists lose sight of the fact that there are many areas of life that bring satisfaction–not just the areas they focus on–and that they don't have to be perfect to have fulfilling lives.

You Are a Work in Progress

The activities in this workbook are invitations to try new things and orient to life in a new way. Scheduling time for mindfulness practice, including mindful awareness in your daily life, and completing exercises designed to increase your understanding of your perfectionism are some of these new things. You will be encouraged to learn to tolerate mistakes, be more accepting of yourself, and become less attached to specific standards.

It will be challenging and uncomfortable to change the habits of thought, behavior, and feeling associated with your perfectionism. It may be tough to become less attached to your specific standards. You may feel uncomfortable trying out new ways to behave, think, and relate to your feelings. Your discomfort may be so great that you may give up at times and resume old habits intentionally or unintentionally. Do not be disturbed by this. In fact, you should expect that you will resume old habits in full force at times. When this happens, instead of being critical of yourself, aim to spend shorter and shorter amounts of time in the old habits. The wisdom in idioms like "get back on the horse" and "fall down seven times, get up eight times" are relevant here. You are more resilient than you know. Your desire to change and the continued effort you dedicate to that are the most important ingredients for long-lasting change. You are ever-evolving as a human with the opportunity to learn from every moment to embody and become your best self.

Key Takeaways

In this first chapter, we explored the many facets of perfectionism. We looked at some of the experiences that are risk factors for perfectionism, the domains in which it presents itself, and the common characteristics of perfectionists. We also considered how the pursuit of excellence is different from perfectionism. Most important, we determined that you are not alone—research published in 2019 in *Psychological Bulletin* indicates that the experience of perfectionism is increasing across the globe. Some key takeaways from this chapter are:

→ Perfectionism is complex and has many facets.

→ A core feature of perfectionism is rigidly holding excessively high standards tied to your self-worth.

→ Perfectionism presents itself uniquely in each person.

→ Problematic perfectionism can be distinguished from the pursuit of excellence and high standards. You don't have to give up your pursuit of high standards to work on your perfectionism.

→ Your perfectionism may be present in one or more life domains.

→ It is useful to understand your particular variety of perfectionism and how it may cause problems.

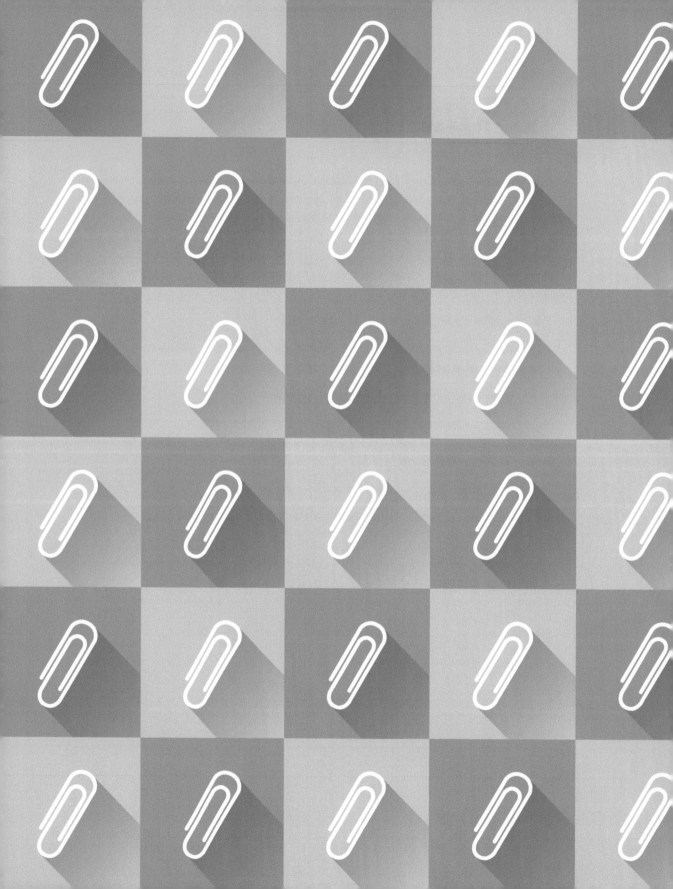

Introduction to Mindfulness

During the past twenty-five years, the word "mindfulness" has been seemingly everywhere. It's often touted as an antidote to a long list of human problems—from dealing with cancer to increasing corporate productivity. But not everyone has the same definition of mindfulness. Criticisms of what is presented as mindfulness and who counts as an expert on it are valid. The reality is that there are many definitions of mindfulness. One of the reasons I believe it has become so popular is because it embodies wisdom that has evolved over generations of human consciousness, and it stimulates a richness and connection with life that many crave in contemporary society.

In this chapter, I provide a clear description of mindfulness in contemporary terms, reflecting on how it has been translated for use in our modern disciplines of healing. The view of mindfulness that I present comes from the discipline that I know best: contemporary psychological practice. This will give you a foundation for your exploration of mindful awareness, or mindfulness, as a way to relate differently to your perfectionistic mind. But please keep in mind that, while I hope the information is helpful, it isn't a substitute for the disciplined, unparalleled coaching you can receive from a mindfulness teacher immersed in any number of traditions.

JADEN EMBRACES MINDFULNESS

Jaden, a physician completing a residency in a competitive program, took great pride in their stellar record of achievement. Jaden was at the top of their class, entered an exclusive liberal arts college, and attended a top medical school. But outstanding grades, standardized test scores in the top 5 percent, and all their other achievements had not brought the happiness they expected. As a self-described workaholic, Jaden devoted most of their time to becoming a physician. They spent much effort fulfilling the expectations of their parent, family, teachers, and colleagues, believing that being on top was the way to being respected. Jaden's self-worth was 100 percent related to these achievements. Then a diagnostic mistake—though it wasn't fatal to the patient—sent Jaden reeling into a mini-crisis. Jaden began to constantly check their decision-making, seek reassurance, and worry about the next error, and they often felt tense and uptight. A trusted colleague who had developed his own mindfulness practice suggested psychotherapy and mindfulness to deal with stress. Jaden reluctantly began a process of self-discovery but skeptically questioned every description of mindfulness. Jaden typically responded to worry about making mistakes by working harder and could not grasp the idea of just observing and accepting those thoughts. Jaden finally related to the phrase "just because you think it, doesn't mean it's true," while at the same time finally experiencing a calming of their mind and body during mindful breathing. Gradually they experimented with various mindfulness apps and podcasts and later became open to processing traumatic events in psychotherapy.

What Is Mindfulness?

Dr. Jon Kabat-Zinn, the founder of mindfulness-based stress reduction (MBSR) decades before the term mindfulness became ubiquitous, is worth quoting here:

> "Mindfulness is awareness. My operational definition of mindfulness is that it is the awareness that arises from paying attention on purpose, in the present moment, and nonjudgmentally. If you need a reason for doing so, we

could add in the service of wisdom, self-understanding, and recognizing our intrinsic interconnections with others and the world, and thus, also in the service of kindness and compassion."

Mindfulness is a practice, in the sense that it involves specific strategies or methods, but it's much more than any one method or compilation of methods. It is a state of mind or attitude. It also includes fundamental ways of seeing the world and life. It involves an ongoing process of learning how to *be*, or *being* rather than *doing*. It's a process or journey and not an outcome. Perfectionists, who focus on *doing* to attain the outcomes essential to their sense of self-worth, benefit from this practice, which in some respects is the opposite of the crux of perfectionistic suffering. Mindfulness transforms your relationship to yourself, your thoughts, and your feelings. Above all, its benefits have been proven by many different practitioners, sages, and scientific studies.

As with any practice, mindfulness must be repeated over time to be of benefit. It may be cultivated through formal practices such as a seated meditation, walking meditation, or yoga, but there are thousands of specific mindfulness practices. Each person must develop a set of practices that works for them. This will involve not only identifying your preferred techniques but also embodying the attitude or state of mind associated with mindfulness. Jon Kabat-Zinn's description of the seven pillars of mindfulness, described in the pages that follow, is a helpful way to convey in words this state of mind.

Where Mindfulness Came From, Where It Is Today

Modern-day mindfulness evolved from ancient, thousands-years-old Buddhist traditions and teachings originating on the Asian continent. Although mindfulness has roots in spiritual training from the East, you don't need to adopt any spiritual practice or belief system to develop a mindfulness practice. In recognition of the benefits, modern-day healers—psychologists, physicians, and others—have been translating the essence of the ancient teachings into more accessible and contemporary skills.

Jon Kabat-Zinn pioneered the the use of mindfulness techniques more than forty years ago at the University of Massachusetts Medical Center to help individuals with various physical illnesses deal with the stress and impact on their physical and emotional well-being resulting from their diagnosis. Physicians referred individuals to Kabat-Zinn's eight-week mindfulness training program, then called the Stress Reduction and Relaxation program. This was the precursor to mindfulness-based stress reduction, which is now a proven treatment for many ailments. Other psychologists began to translate ancient practices into contemporary mindfulness approaches for healing and scientifically evaluated their effectiveness, including Marsha Linehan, the originator of dialectical behavior therapy (DBT), and Steven Hayes, the originator of acceptance and commitment therapy (ACT). The cultivation of mindfulness skills is now included in a number of other evidence-based treatments, including mindfulness-based cognitive therapy (MBCT). Each application emphasizes different essential features of mindfulness practice and uses different language to explain similar ideas.

Contemporary psychological science recognizes mindfulness as a "capacity of mind"—that is, the ability to be present, focused, and aware and accepting of internal experience. When we study mindfulness from this perspective, it becomes apparent that some people naturally have a greater capacity of mind than others, and that deficits in this capacity relate to or compound a number of psychological difficulties. Low levels of mindfulness have been found in perfectionists.

The Seven Pillars

Jon Kabat-Zinn identified seven pillars or attitudes toward mindfulness practice: beginner's mind, nonjudgment, acceptance, patience, trust, non-striving, and letting go. He also emphasized that generosity and gratitude further enhance mindfulness as a practice. You can think of these seven pillars as the essential supporting structures of a house. Without them, the house would be at risk of collapsing. In any mindfulness practice, these pillars form the essential structure necessary for strong, sustained impact.

Beginner's Mind

This is the capacity to see things as if for the first time—as if you're starting from scratch, from a place of not knowing or not expecting a particular outcome. In a beginner's mind, you are free from your expectations of how things should be.

When we have expectations of how things should be, we miss important aspects of what is happening right before our eyes. Some people describe this attitude as seeing the way a naive child would. It's a way of looking at the world with awe, anticipation, and openness to what evolves.

Nonjudgment

Most people are socialized to judge and categorize what is acceptable and good and what is not. In a stance of nonjudgment, there is an attempt to suspend learned categorizations of what is good and what is not. This stance is one in which you prioritize noticing, not evaluating or judging. You simply engage your mind to observe thoughts, feelings, and emotions. A stance of nonjudgment is one of neutrality. You observe your experiences inside and outside of yourself, tolerating and coexisting with these experiences without judging their merits. For perfectionists, any thought or behavior not previously conceived as serving the standard is considered problematic, making nonjudgment especially difficult to master.

Acceptance

Many people resist dealing with what actually happens. Especially when they believe what actually happens is not ideal. It is particularly difficult to tolerate negative emotions and experiences that don't fit preconceived ideas about what is necessary and good. It is easier to accept positive experiences, emotions, and outcomes. In a stance of acceptance, you embrace everything and become tolerant of experiences that are desirable as well as those that aren't. In this state, you neutrally notice and coexist with experiences that are positive and negative, expected and surprising.

Patience

Patience is complete openness to each moment, knowing and accepting that things evolve in a time frame that cannot be controlled or predicted. It is antithetical to perfectionists who want to be assured of what will happen when. It is also antithetical to wanting to control what will happen. A stance of patience recognizes that things evolve in their own time and that we must be patient to observe the timing of that evolution.

Trust

Only you can be the authority on you, what you are experiencing, and what is right for you. Attunement and recognition of the wisdom in your own experience is the essence of trust. A stance of trust acknowledges that, ultimately, you are the only one who can really know what is right for you. It involves including the perspectives of others but at the same time trusting yourself and your innate wisdom. In mindfulness, this means that you will be the one deciding what works for you. Above all, it recognizes the essential worthiness of you, independent of any other person's opinion or of what you have been able to accomplish.

Non-Striving

Non-striving refers to the attitude of allowing things to be the way they are without concern for the outcome. This attitude is particularly difficult to master if you strive for specific goals and standards. Contemporary life pulls us to be purposeful and goal-oriented, whether we are perfectionists or not. With the non-striving attitude, you simply pay attention to the present. This is perhaps the attitude best described by the word "non-doing." You pay attention to the present moment, observing whatever is happening and focusing equally on negative, positive, and neutral experiences.

Letting Go

This involves cultivating the attitude of non-attachment. As humans, we tend to overfocus on certain thoughts and feelings. Mindful awareness helps us identify those thoughts and feelings that we tend to hold on to. This attitude is the opposite of clinging and resists the tendency to hold on to certain thoughts, emotions, feelings, or sensations. Instead, you aim to give all your experiences the same level of attention. This might be especially difficult for perfectionists because when you stop and become aware the negative self-talk, it's harder to ignore your internal pressure to pursue high standards.

Additional Principles: Generosity and Gratitude

Generosity and gratitude are other fruitful states of mind to cultivate as you develop the capacity to become present and aware in the moment. Generosity involves giving freely to yourself and others while expecting nothing in return. It's about recognizing your positive qualities and gifts and sharing them freely. These gifts include your best self, enthusiasm, spirit, openness, trust, and presence, but also freely practicing self-acceptance. Once we are accustomed to providing these to ourselves and feel deserving of them, it becomes natural to extend these gifts to others.

Gratitude involves noticing small positive things that we take for granted but that are nevertheless associated with our well-being. As we increase our awareness, we can bring appreciation and gratitude to the present moment. Noticing the goodness in our lives has a snowball effect that enhances overall well-being.

Generosity and gratitude are not neutral frames of mind. Traditionally, mindfulness was taught alongside other practices, such as generosity, gratitude, kindness, and compassion, to cultivate positive states of mind. There are specific practices to cultivate these qualities, and they may be seen as enhancements to the foundational practices. Psychological science has established clear evidence of the benefits of cultivating gratitude, compassion, and self-compassion.

What Mindfulness Is Not

Many myths and misunderstandings about mindfulness exist. In the following list, I describe what mindfulness is not. On the next pages, I present a more reality-based description of what it is.

- **Mindfulness is not only formal meditation or seated meditation.** It is optimally cultivated through formal meditation, but it is not synonymous with meditation. All meditation, however, includes the practice of mindfulness. Mindfulness includes many different practices and is above all a state of mind.

- **Mindfulness is not an emptying of your mind.** It is impossible to not think or feel. Mindfulness shifts your relationship to your thoughts, feelings, and memories. You develop the ability to be aware, open, and accepting to here-and-now experiences (thoughts, feelings, memories, immediate surroundings), observing them without judging them.

- **Mindfulness is not just a technique or method.** It is a way of existing, being, or relating to your inner world and the world outside you.

- **Mindfulness is not a cure-all.** It has many benefits and can be transformative, but it is rarely a stand-alone method for lasting change, especially for those with mental health concerns.

- **Mindfulness is not a religious or spiritual practice.** A related myth is that mindfulness teachers, especially those with connections to ancient traditions, are secretly on a mission to convert others. Mindfulness evolved from Buddhist spiritual practices but is compatible with any number of religious practices.

- **Mindfulness is not a focus exclusively on yourself.** Mindfulness practices cultivate connection and relationship to yourself and the world around you.

- **Mindfulness is not a way to escape from your problems or to achieve a blissful state of mind.** Instead, the practice helps you become more engaged and aware in your day-to-day life.

Mindfulness Is for Everyone

Everyone has the capacity to cultivate a mindfulness practice because it relies on basic mental processes. Although the unique set of mechanisms responsible for mindfulness's effects have yet to be identified, we know the core components.

The core mental processes involved include focusing and regulating attention. We could call this concentration, or the "learned control of the focus of attention." Mindfulness also relies on observation, which, in cognitive psychology, is often referred to as metacognition or the capacity to think about one's thinking. The capacity for metacognition develops in early childhood. Mindfulness also relies on the cognitive process of appraisal, which is the process of deriving meaning from our experiences. In mindfulness practice, as we observe our experience (thoughts, feelings, and physical sensations), we move toward an appraisal that is not judgmental but neutral and accepting. Mindfulness is accessible to everyone because normal developing humans, including children, possess these basic mental processes.

Mindfulness Is Evidence-Based and Effective

Mindfulness has been researched extensively, both as a skill that can be learned and practiced and as a capacity of mind or dispositional characteristic. As a skill, some studies have determined its effectiveness in the treatment of specific mental health conditions, as well as increasing the health and well-being in nonclinical populations (those who do not have mental health diagnoses). As a dispositional characteristic, studies have established that low capacity for mindfulness is associated with worry, rumination, a range of symptoms seen in mental health disorders, and more distress. Two recent studies published in the *Journal of Clinical Psychology* and the *Journal of Contextual Behavioral Science* established that socially prescribed perfectionism and perfectionistic self-presentation are associated with low mindfulness.

A number of methods have been used to study mindfulness, including self-report questionnaires, experimental inductions, neurophysiological measures, mindfulness training interventions, and comparison of expert practitioners to others. Several meta-analyses (pooled results of independent studies that determine overall statistical significance) conducted in recent years have determined that mindfulness-based interventions such as MBSR, MBCT, DBT, and compassion-focused approaches are effective at reducing anxiety, stress, and relapses of depression. A 2016 meta-analysis of studies conducted on nonclinical populations published in *Psychotherapy and Psychosomatics* concluded that MBSR and MBCT reduced worry, stress, depression, and anxiety. Meta-analyses of DBT have indicated it is an effective treatment for reducing suicidal behavior. Meta-analyses of MBSR, perhaps the most studied mindfulness intervention, indicate it has a moderately large positive effect on mental health, somatic health, and quality of life. In general, the research on mindfulness-based interventions demonstrates that they are equivalent to established evidence-based interventions.

The Positive Effects of Mindfulness

Mindfulness-based interventions have been found to reduce many forms of psychological distress, including generalized anxiety disorder, social anxiety disorder, relapse in those with recurrent depression, anger, attention-deficit/hyperactivity disorder, and parasuicidal behavior.

Research published in *Personality and Social Psychology* and *Cognitive, Affective, & Behavioral Neuroscience* documented that, in addition to alleviating mental health concerns, training in mindfulness improves a number of outcomes, including immune function, cognitive decline, sleep, burnout, mood, and heart health.

Focused treatment of perfectionism and the evaluation of such targeted treatment is in its infancy. Cognitive behavioral therapy (not mindfulness-based) for perfectionism is the most studied intervention and has been demonstrated to be effective. Development and evaluation of mindfulness-based interventions for perfectionism are in the early stages, but pilot studies of ACT for clinical perfectionism, MBCT for perfectionism, and mindful compassion for perfectionism in personality disorder show promising results. The 2020 MBCT pilot study published in *Bollettino di Psicologia Applicata* (*Applied Psychology Bulletin*) compared it with a CBT-derived self-help guide. MBCT was superior in changing daily impairment caused by perfectionism, unhelpful beliefs about emotions, rumination, mindfulness, self-compassion, and decentering. A 2020 study, published in the journal *Psychophysiology*, of college-age perfectionists who were experiencing experimentally derived failure indicated that mindfulness meditation focusing on nonjudgment of emotion was effective in improving heart rate variability, a measure of ability to recover from stress.

Mindfulness Tools

As discussed previously, mindfulness practice is one aspect of cultivating mindfulness. Over time, you will build a toolbox of practices that match your preferences and lifestyle. The contents of this toolbox will likely include stand-alone practices such as seated meditation, walking meditation, mindful movement, or yoga that can be used during specific blocks of time to train your awareness. But it will also include shorter practices that may be used on an ongoing basis throughout your daily life. Most important, the toolbox you build will help you understand and employ the seven structural supports of beginner's mind, nonjudgment, acceptance, patience, trust, non-striving, and letting go. In the second part of the book, you will find a discussion of tools organized according to these structural supporting attitudes.

Beginning a Mindfulness Practice

Mindfulness is a skill, which means it takes repetition and practice. Like riding a bicycle or attaining expert performance, you must use the skill over and over again before you reap the rewards of your efforts. Each attempt at practice will give you information to use on your next attempt. Don't expect miraculous results the first time you try a practice or exercise. In fact, be open to the effects that may be small, negligible, or barely discernable. This means that you must commit to sustained practice of a particular tool, which will likely be frustrating. I often tell my clients that if it were as simple as telling/describing to people what they should do, there would be no need for psychologists or the myriad individuals who have invested their lives in understanding how to help people change.

It may be helpful to know that the process of change is complex and has been studied and documented. In order to change, it's important for you to understand the circumstances associated with your difficulties, discover the tools that help, and use these tools regularly. It's also important to anticipate times when you'll revert to self-defeating behaviors–these relapses are to be expected and are opportunities to learn what to do differently next time. Perfectionists who cling to positive outcomes may struggle with not having a clear positive result and with reverting to old patterns. These instances are likely to be your most potent teachers.

Why Mindfulness Is Good for Managing Perfectionism

Mindfulness is a good match for perfectionism because it targets aspects of what makes perfectionism problematic. In perfectionism, there is often much judgment and criticism of yourself and others. Mindfulness practice involves teaching the perfectionist to approach experiences without judgment. In perfectionism, high standards for performance become the main focus of the individual's efforts. Mindfulness practice teaches the perfectionist to resist fixating on outcomes. Learning to detach from a particular outcome, accepting the experience as it is, and allowing the experience to evolve counteracts compulsive striving for goals, which is common in perfectionism. Trust also helps shift your focus from a specific goal to the present moment, while patience and letting go are antidotes to the perfectionist criticisms of self and others.

Expect Imperfection

Learning mindfulness is challenging. Expect an uneven pace when you are changing ingrained habits related to your perfectionism. Expect yourself to feel unsure. Expect yourself to complete only some of the exercises and practices as described. At times you will feel frustrated and may want to give up entirely. If you do become frustrated and leave the work for a couple of days, come back to it. Take small steps. Learning the practices and reaping the benefits of mindfulness practice will take time. Be patient with yourself. Above all, do not expect perfection. Embrace imperfection.

Key Takeaways

In this chapter, we explored how mindfulness practices have existed as an aid to human suffering for thousands of years and have been proven effective by modern-day research. We also looked at the benefits of mindfulness, research supporting its efficacy, and the seven pillars of mindfulness. Key takeaways from this chapter include:

→ Mindfulness can be cultivated by everyone.

→ Mindfulness is a practice that can be cultivated through scheduled practices, but is most helpful when brought to your daily life.

→ Mindfulness practices have been demonstrated effective in many scientific studies.

→ Mindfulness is antithetical to perfectionism, so it will likely be challenging for you.

→ To obtain the benefits of mindfulness, you must practice it as you would any other skill.

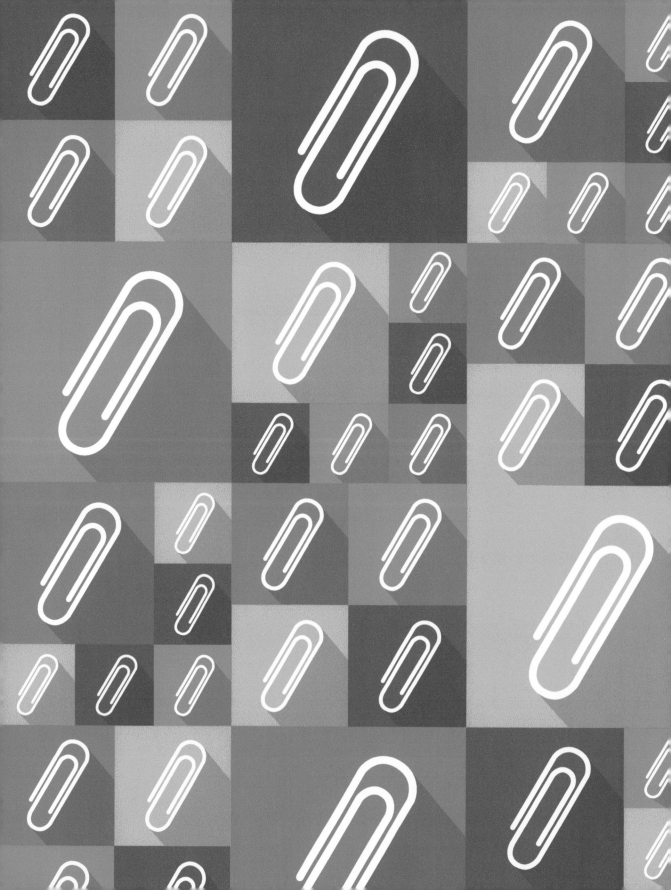

Practicing Mindfulness to Overcome Perfectionism

The second part of this book is divided into seven chapters, each providing mindfulness-based practices organized by the seven pillars of mindfulness: beginner's mind, non-judgment, acceptance, patience, trust, non-striving, and letting go. Each chapter contains methods to engage a calm, nonjudgmental awareness rather than the anxiety and rumination your perfectionism brings. Each chapter also contains prompts and exercises to build your awareness of the factors associated with your perfectionism. These exercises and prompts are another way to step back, observe, shift, and gain perspective on not only perfectionism-driven thoughts, feelings, and behaviors but also the impact you have on others, the impact others have on you, and what is really important for a vital, meaningful life.

Increasing your awareness of the problems perfectionism causes for you and trying new practices while observing their impact on your life is a powerful recipe for change. Ultimately, these practices will enable you to develop a healthy attitude that will help you achieve what is important to you. As you work through these chapters, please release any expectation of doing them perfectly or attaining a perfect outcome. Some of the exercises will be useful and some will not. Make an effort, acknowledge your effort, acknowledge the helpful things, acknowledge the things that aren't a good match, then continue on.

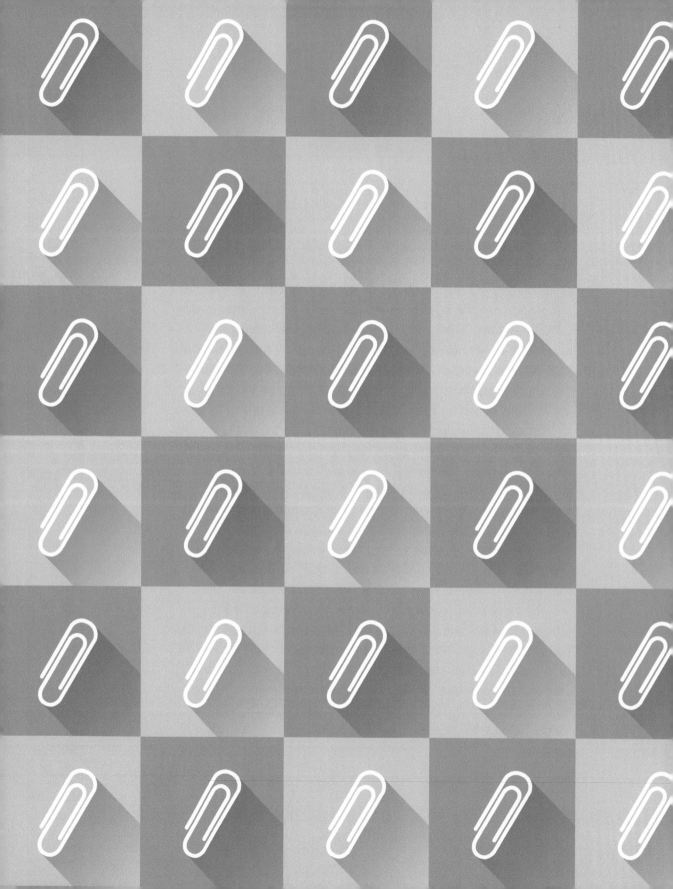

Beginner's Mind: Embracing a New Perspective

Beginner's mind asks that you bring a fresh, novel, open perspective to your brand of perfectionism. This is a difficult idea to embrace for many reasons, including the fact that, as humans, we bring our prior experiences to each current moment. So, how can you be asked to bring a new perspective to a situation with the baggage of the past in tow? One way to think about this is to imagine that you are putting on a lens—a beginner's lens—to improve your vision. As with glasses or contacts, this lens is an enhancement to your existing eyes and body. This beginner's mind lens is especially difficult for those who have a clear image of what they want and what is necessary to make it come to fruition. The lens doesn't ignore this image; rather, it focuses on what is happening now. With this lens, you are taking in any situation with openness and curiosity. You see things not as you think they should be or ought to be but as they really are—and you are liberated from any expectations based on your past experiences. In this chapter you will look closely at your perfectionism to clarify how it may create difficulties for you.

VAN SEES LIFE IN A NEW LIGHT

Van, a mother of two teen boys, had been anxious since her own teen years. She came to therapy after experiencing a panic attack at work after worrying constantly about her sons' well-being. She had always been one to achieve at the high level demanded by her immigrant parents. But while the pressure she put on herself to perform had always seemed manageable, lately she became more worried about making mistakes at work and as a parent. She felt little joy, began experiencing more sleepless nights, and was simply not satisfied with her life. When one of her sons began to rebel against her constant nagging and told her he hated her, she decided to seek help. At first, the thought of including mindfulness practices seemed alien. It was too "woo-woo," she said. But the idea of looking at her life with a new perspective seemed less weird. At first, she found it difficult to schedule time for the practices, and some days she did nothing at all. On other days, she found fifteen to thirty minutes to try them, and her once-frenzied mind began to settle and calm. She gained new insights about her need for her sons to excel and how her relentless pursuit of certain achievements had deprived her of joy. To her surprise, she began to feel more in control, less dysregulated, and less overwhelmed. She began to relinquish the control she thought she had over her sons' lives and developed more hope about their future and her own.

Mindful Breathing

Cultivating awareness of your breathing is fundamental to mindfulness practice. It's also a tool that's accessible to everyone, as we all breathe and our breath is always with us. You can bring awareness to your breath as a stand-alone practice, devoting several minutes a day, or you may use it throughout the day when you notice an uptick in your stress level. Cultivating a mindful breathing stand-alone practice will help you learn to use it whenever necessary.

Focus your attention on your breath. Don't attempt to change it, just notice it. Gently notice your inhale and exhale. Notice how your inhale may be different from your exhale. Notice how the air enters your nostrils and your lungs. Tune in completely to your breath. If thoughts come up, simply allow them to pass. You may notice discomfort in parts of your body. If so, note the discomfort and reorient to the air entering and leaving your body. As you continue, you'll begin to hear sounds outside of you that you weren't previously aware of. Notice these and come back to noticing your breath. Do this for three to five minutes.

The Double-Edged Sword of Perfectionism

Perfectionism is complex. It becomes prominent because aspects of it function to serve you well. In contrast, there are dark, shadow aspects that hurt and cause pain. Full illumination is a step toward growth and healing. Relax, take a breath, and write stream of consciousness responses—meaning without hesitation or editing—to the following prompts:

Perfectionism has helped me: _____

_____

_____

Perfectionism has hurt me or caused me pain: _____

_____

_____

My perfectionism has caused the following problems for others: _____

_____

_____

Forms of Perfectionism

Let's take some time to reflect on which of the three forms of perfectionism described in chapter 1 are part of your pattern. If you check several statements related to one of the forms, it is likely relevant for you.

Self-Oriented Perfectionism

In this pattern, you set lofty goals or standards for yourself and become very critical when you do not meet these goals or standards. At times, you may see yourself as flawed and weak, but you guard against appearing imperfect. You are likely to be disciplined, conscientious, persistent, responsible, organized, detailed, and efficient but you may be plagued by self-doubt. Check each statement that applies to you:

☐ I would like to be perfect in everything I do.

☐ I strive to be the best in everything I do.

☐ I have very high standards for myself.

☐ I get uneasy or upset when I make mistakes.

☐ I must give my full effort to everything I do.

☐ It is important for me to be successful at work, home, or school.

Other-Oriented Perfectionism

In this pattern, you expect others to conform to high goals and standards. When they do not meet these standards, you may become angry and unsympathetic. You might prefer to do things yourself so that they are done to your liking. You may be aware that others see you as never being satisfied with what they do. You tell them what to do and how to do it, put them down, and are generally very critical and blaming. Check each statement that applies to you:

☐ I have high standards for those people who are important to me.

☐ It upsets me when others around me do not do their best.

☐ I prefer to avoid people who set low standards for themselves.

☐ I expect a lot from my friends.

☐ If I ask someone to do something, I expect it to be done flawlessly.

☐ I demand the same perfection from others that I do of myself.

Socially Prescribed Perfectionism

In this pattern, you believe that others have exceedingly high standards for you that they are consistently judging you on. You attempt to meet these standards because you want others to like you and not reject you. At times, you will do what you believe others wish you to do and, as a result, may feel victimized and resentful of others and their perceived demands. Check each statement that applies to you:

☐ Others will not like or respect me if I do not excel.

☐ People will get upset if I make mistakes.

☐ I find it difficult to meet others' expectations of me.

☐ If I do anything short of exceptional, others will see it as unacceptable.

☐ People will not accept me if I don't succeed.

☐ People expect more from me than I can deliver.

Domains of Perfectionism

For some people, perfectionism presents itself across all areas of life. In others, perfectionism may present in only one or a few domains–for example, a naturally gifted musician aiming for celebrity status who put minimal effort into school and college, appearance, friendships, and physical health but is a perfectionist about their practice. Determine the domain(s) in which your perfectionism presents, then indicate where your standards fall in relation to other people you know by drawing a star on the corresponding line. There are a few extra lines for you to write in domains that are specific to you.

Personal Standards Relative to Others

Domain	LOW	EQUAL TO OTHERS	HIGH
		———————————	———————————	
Academics and School		———————————	———————————	
Parenting		———————————	———————————	

Professional Life		————————	————————	
Health and Fitness		————————	————————	
Romantic Relationships		————————	————————	
Social Life		————————	————————	
_____		————————	————————	
_____		————————	————————	
_____		————————	————————	

The Image You Present to the World

Many perfectionists put a lot of effort into their public image. They put energy into making sure that others see a flawless, perfect version of themselves. There are three facets of this self-presentation: curating and presenting an ideal image, keeping guard to avoid slipping up and showing their imperfection, and never discussing mistakes or flaws with others. If these tendencies sound familiar it means that you are presenting your ideal self to the world and not your true self. The following statements are based on the Perfectionistic Self-Presentation Scale. Select the statement that seems true for you in each checklist:

Promoting an Image of Perfection

☐ I make sure to talk about my accomplishments.

☐ I make sure to have all the things that show the world I am a success (fancy clothes, car, vacations).

☐ I must always seem in control.

☐ I must always be flawlessly groomed.

☐ I must seem perfect (competent, on top of things, virtuous, etc.) for others to accept me.

Avoiding Showing Imperfection

☐ I get distraught if I make a mistake that others notice.

☐ I try to hide my mistakes.

☐ I don't do anything that I am not sure will be perfect.

☐ It is much worse to make a mistake that others know about.

☐ I am devastated if others see me as less than perfect.

Keeping Imperfections Hidden

☐ I keep my worries and problems to myself.

☐ I try to fix issues on my own.

☐ I don't discuss my mistakes with anyone.

☐ I avoid admitting that I was wrong.

☐ I don't discuss my fears with anyone.

Body Scan Meditation

The body scan meditation is a stand-alone practice that you can do for varying lengths of time. Here I describe a relatively brief version of the practice that will take fifteen to thirty minutes.

There are many scripts and guided body scan meditation practices available, so you can also research free guided practices if you think you may prefer a voice to guide you initially. You can do a body scan while sitting, standing, or lying down. These instructions assume you are lying down.

1. Find a comfortable, quiet place to lie down and close your eyes.

2. Take a few longer inhales and exhales. You will be focusing your attention on different parts of your body, starting with your feet and going up to the crown of your head. As you focus on different body parts, imagine that your attention is like a laser, orienting to and noticing every sensation occurring inside and outside your skin.

3. Start with your toes. Notice how your toes feel in space and in any covering such as socks. Notice temperature and sensations such as tingling, tension, or even pain. Check in with each toe.

4. Next, move on to your feet. Again, your attention is like a laser, homing in on every sensation that appears in your feet.

5. Notice your legs. Notice how your legs feel against the surface you are lying on. Notice every sensation that occurs inside your skin and outside your skin.

6. Move up your body and notice the sensations in your buttocks and stomach. Notice all sensations, inside and outside the skin.

7. Bring your attention to your waist and back. Notice all sensations, inside and outside the skin.

8. Notice your chest and lungs. Notice your breath and how it is entering and exiting your body.

9. Notice your hands, arms, and shoulders. Notice all sensations, inside and outside the skin.

10. Notice your neck, throat, jaw, lips, nose, eyes, and eyebrows. Notice all sensations, inside and outside the skin.

11. Notice the crown of your head.

12. Repeat this, starting from your toes and progressing to the top of your head, two or three times or more until it seems appropriate to stop.

Ways of Thinking Associated with Your Perfectionism (Automatic Perfectionistic Thoughts)

Use the following checklist to identify patterns of thinking associated with your perfectionism. Automatic thoughts comprise the stream of self-talk that occurs in our minds, often in the background, until we acknowledge the thoughts and pay attention to them. Start paying attention to these thoughts to become more conscious of your perfectionism. Over time, becoming more attuned, aware, and attentive to these thoughts will help you recognize how they affect your moods, emotions, and behavior. Some common automatic thoughts reported by those who are perfectionistic are listed here. Check all that apply to you and use the blank spaces to write in some other automatic thoughts that are relevant for you.

- ☐ I must do things perfectly.
- ☐ I must not fail.
- ☐ I can't have others think poorly of me.
- ☐ If I try, then I will only fail.
- ☐ If I make a mistake, I will be rejected.
- ☐ If I put my work out there, others will think badly of me.
- ☐ I must know what is going to happen.
- ☐ I must be prepared for possible outcomes.

- ☐ I can't let anyone else do a task in case it goes wrong.
- ☐ If I don't strive to achieve higher standards, I am worthless.
- ☐ I must work all the time or I will become lazy.
- ☐ _____
- ☐ _____
- ☐ _____
- ☐ _____

Hand-on-Heart

This is a practice you can use whenever you notice your self-critical internal chatter arising or when you feel under stress.

1. Take two or three deep, satisfying breaths.

2. Gently place your hand over your heart, feeling the gentle pressure and warmth of your hand.

3. Try placing both hands on your chest, noticing the difference between one and two hands.

4. Focus all your awareness on the sensations of your palms touching your body. Sometimes it's more effective to put your hands inside your shirt so that you feel your skin.

5. Feel the touch of your hand on your chest–try making small circles with your hand and tune in to the rise and fall of your chest as you breathe in and out.

Self-Defeating Behaviors Associated with Your Perfectionism

There are patterns of behavior often linked with perfectionism, some of which appear in the following checklist. Make a mental note of those patterns you already know cause you distress or are problematic. Place a checkmark next to the ones that describe ways you may behave more often than not.

- ☐ Avoidance
- ☐ Procrastination
- ☐ Checking your performance
- ☐ Problems making decisions
- ☐ Seeking reassurance
- ☐ Giving up too soon
- ☐ Not knowing when to stop

- ☐ Overcompensating
- ☐ Going painfully slowly to avoid mistakes
- ☐ Doing everything yourself and not asking for help
- ☐ Only doing what you know you are very good at

Beauty in Imperfection

I have a beautiful ceramic bowl veined with irregular stripes of gold that sits on my bookshelf. It was created using the ancient Japanese art form of Kintsugi. In this centuries-old process, broken pottery is repaired using a binding material dusted with actual gold. The end result is a piece of pottery that doesn't hide where the breaks occurred but instead overlays them with gold to produce a piece that is unique and even more beautiful and precious than it was before. Kintsugi is a metaphor for embracing the raw, broken parts of ourselves and seeing them as aspects of our perfectly imperfect beauty. I encourage you to search for images of Kintsugi pottery on the internet and keep a few of those images in mind as you answer the following prompts.

What experiences come up as you think about this concept? _____

_____

_____

_____

_____

What emotions do you notice? _____

_____

_____

_____

_____

What do you take with you related to your perfectionism? _____

_____

_____

_____

_____

Why Be Different and What Will Help?

This exercise will clarify your desire to change and help you feel more confident about making those changes. There are likely things outside of you, as well as things about you, that will both hinder and help you on this journey. Use the first matrix to identify reasons to change and to not change. Use the second to identify barriers and supporters of change. When the barriers and arguments against change come up, simply notice the irritation or other negative emotion arising.

	INTERNAL	EXTERNAL
Reasons to Change		
Reasons Not to Change		

	INTERNAL	EXTERNAL
Barriers to Change		
Supporters of Change		

Key Takeaways

The essence of beginner's mind is to bring a new perspective to your experience. In this chapter, we completed prompts, practices, and exercises designed to bring you a new understanding of how your perfectionism manifests. You examined your perfectionism from many angles: the forms it takes, the domains in which it presents itself, ways of thinking associated with your perfectionism, self-defeating behaviors associated with it, and how you may present an image of yourself to the world because of it. Understanding the factors associated with your perfectionism is an important step toward change. This is the very start of your journey to mindful awareness. Remember these key takeaways from this chapter:

→ Understand your version of perfectionism.

→ Imperfection is real and has beauty.

→ Affirm your desire to change.

→ Acknowledge the factors that make it difficult to change.

→ Keep using the practices.

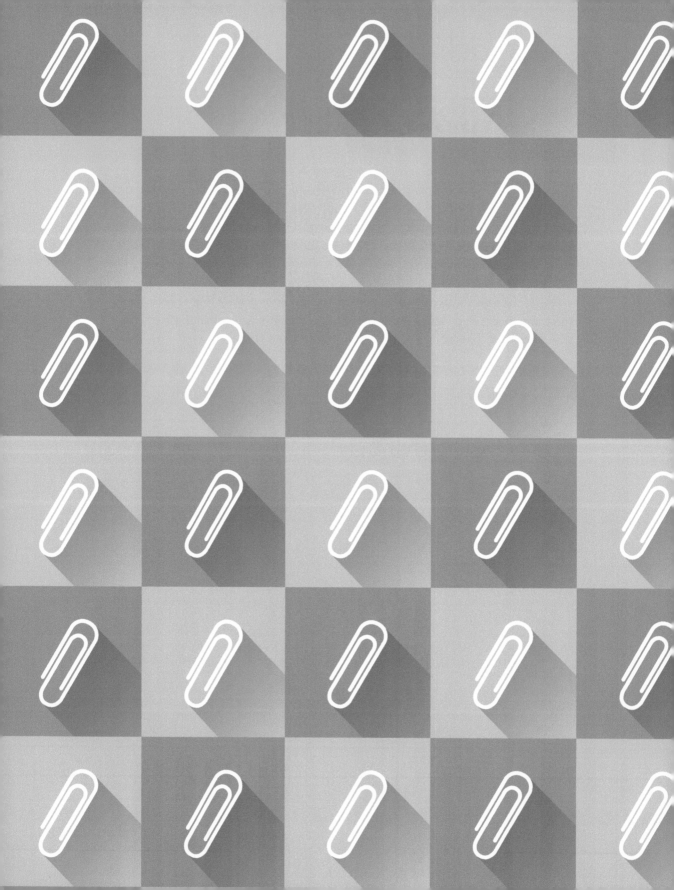

Nonjudgment: Stepping Back from Your Inner Critic

"Y ou messed up. This is not good enough. You won't make it." These words are no doubt familiar. It's that critical internal voice that's always monitoring and evaluating you and is constantly on guard to point out when you fall short of your expectations and goals. It tells you that you're weak, inadequate, and flawed. This critical viewpoint may not only be directed at yourself, but also at family, friends, and others you meet in your daily life.

"Nonjudgment" means refraining from evaluation, and it is contrary to perfectionism. Practicing this attitude will be especially difficult because, when you become still, that critical voice gets louder and harder to ignore. In this chapter, you will find exercises to observe and quiet that internal critic, including mindfulness practices to train nonjudgment and to counter that harsh criticism. In response to your self-talk, you will practice shifting your attention from blaming and shaming to a neutral response, then a kind and compassionate one. You will also find exercises to increase your understanding of your critical self and develop a more complete view of yourself.

DAN'S INTERNAL CRITIC—FRIEND OR FOE?

Dan knew he had to do something different when he got free tickets for March Madness and had no one to go with. As a sales manager, he had spent the past fifteen years advancing up the corporate ladder, and his team consistently outperformed all others. He worked long hours and demanded the same from his team members. Outstanding performance motivated him to continue to exceed performance targets. To do so, he required his team members to check in with him weekly about their goals. If he was not pleased with the results, he would take over himself. He was aware that his team considered him a micromanager and that they had the most turnover of any team in the division, but he chalked that up to others not being able to live up to his standards and blamed them. When he began to reflect on his life, he realized he hadn't been in a romantic relationship for five years and for the first time began to acknowledge his loneliness. He wasn't aware of the downside of his internal monologue. At first, he believed that his inner speech was actually the thing to which he could attribute his success. Thoughts that told him he could fail and be humiliated motivated him, made him tougher, and made him a better person. But as he looked at his life, Dan began to see how his self-worth was tied entirely to his job performance, that he was unhappy, and that he wanted more out of life.

My Inner Critic: What Is It Saying?

Let us stop, pause, and look at what the inner critic is preoccupied with. Drs. Gordon Flett, Paul Hewitt, Taryn Nepon, and Avi Besser's Perfectionism Cognition Theory comprehensively describes the types of thoughts observed in perfectionists. The following list combines the Perfectionism Cognitions Inventory and other self-reporting measures that capture perfectionists' thoughts.

Please read each thought carefully and indicate how frequently, if at all, the thoughts occurred to you over the *past week*. Circle the appropriate number, using the following scale: 0 = not at all, 1 = sometimes, 2 = moderately often, 3 = often, and 4 = all the time.

I must perform to my standard at all times.	0	1	2	3	4
I need to do better.	0	1	2	3	4
I should be perfect.	0	1	2	3	4
I should never make mistakes.	0	1	2	3	4
I hate to fail at anything.	0	1	2	3	4
I have to be the best.	0	1	2	3	4
I should be doing more.	0	1	2	3	4
I have fallen short of my standards.	0	1	2	3	4
I can't stand to make mistakes.	0	1	2	3	4
I have to work hard all the time.	0	1	2	3	4
No matter how much I do, it's never enough.	0	1	2	3	4
People expect me to be perfect.	0	1	2	3	4
People won't respect me if I am not perfect.	0	1	2	3	4
I am upset because someone else is better at something than I am.	0	1	2	3	4
I must do better.	0	1	2	3	4
If I am not an absolute success, then my life is meaningless.	0	1	2	3	4
Why can't things be perfect?	0	1	2	3	4
My work or performance has to be the best.	0	1	2	3	4
I am afraid I won't do something well.	0	1	2	3	4
My work should be flawless.	0	1	2	3	4
I should always be in complete control of my feelings.	0	1	2	3	4

→

I wonder how others thought about me and my work.	0	1	2	3	4
My value as a person depends on performing at the highest level.	0	1	2	3	4
I made a mistake, so I am a failure as a person.	0	1	2	3	4
If I did not set high standards for myself, I would be a loser.	0	1	2	3	4
Why can't I do the extraordinary things other people do?	0	1	2	3	4
I must be successful.	0	1	2	3	4
I am not as good as other people.	0	1	2	3	4
I have to work harder.	0	1	2	3	4

Observing the Inner Critic

Document the top five thoughts of your inner critic. These will be all the ones that you indicated happened "often" or "all the time" over the last week. Thoughts have power–they prompt feelings and behavior. Observing thoughts is the mindful way. Practice becoming an observer of your top five thoughts by editing them in this exercise to reflect that you are noticing each one rather than reacting to it. Add "I am having the thought that . . ." to preface the thought. See the example.

INNER CRITIC'S THOUGHT

I have to work hard all the time.

OBSERVER'S EDIT

I am having the thought that I have to work hard all the time.

_____   _____

_____   _____

_____   _____

_____   _____

_____   _____

Stay alert for the next time these thoughts occur–they may come up in quick succession. When these thoughts arise during the day, imagine you have edited them and placed them on a teleprompter that you can read in a neutral announcer's voice. This edited stream on the teleprompter may read, "I am having the thought that I have to work all the time. I am having the thought that I will fail. I am having the thought that I must be efficient at all times." This helps you see them without judgment.

STOP

The inner critic is unpleasant. When your inner critic is activated, you may feel stressed out. STOP is a practice that comes from mindfulness-based stress reduction. It is an acronym to guide how–in a moment of stress, tension, or overwhelm–we can choose to provide space to move forward. This quote from psychologist Viktor Frankl captures more eloquently what the steps prescribe:

> *"Between stimulus and response, there is a space. In that space is our power to choose our response. In our response lies our growth and our freedom."*

S - Stop and pause.

T - Take one conscious breath.

O - Observe what is going on in your body and your mind.

P - Proceed with what you were doing.

How Does My Inner Critic Make Me Feel?

Thoughts come with feelings. In the space that follows, write your top five thoughts from the "Observing the Inner Critic" exercise on page 50 and indicate the feelings that come with them. See the example. There are many words to describe feelings. If you'd like to keep it simple, you can choose one from this short list: angry, frustrated, fearful, anxious, disgusted, ashamed, sad, depressed, joyful, happy.

INNER CRITIC'S THOUGHT	FEELINGS
I have to work hard all the time.	Anxious, frustrated
_____	_____
_____	_____
_____	_____
_____	_____
_____	_____

Attending to Shame

Shame is a painful emotion that can arise when things don't go the way we expect and, deep down, we believe it's because we are defective. If we stop to verbalize our internal monologue, it is communicating that we are broken, flawed, or inadequate. Shame arises when we fall short of standards, make mistakes, and compare ourselves with others. All emotions are associated with an action, and with shame, we are inclined to hide. Think of a time when you felt shame and then fill out the following prompts.

I felt shame in the following situation: _____

_____

_____

My inner critic stated: _____

_____

_____

In response, I: _____

_____

_____

Compassion Seated Meditation

Compassion meditation guides you to awaken the compassionate part of yourself. When awakened, this kinder, gentler, wiser part of yourself can help soften the impact of your inner critic by acknowledging how much suffering the criticism brings. When you connect with your own suffering, you can extend this understanding to others. You see your own imperfect humanity, along with that of others, more clearly.

1. Find a comfortable place to sit for ten to fifteen minutes.

2. Get in a comfortable position. Notice yourself being supported by the place you are sitting. There is no perfect way to try this and nothing that you are aiming for.

3. Bring your attention to your breath, inhaling and exhaling three times.

4. Bring loving, kind feelings to yourself. To do this, you may imagine a time, person, or event that you associate with pure love. As you bring this person, event, or time to your mind, notice and heighten the loving feelings.

5. Notice how you feel and where that feeling manifests in your body. This feeling is available to you at any time. Let what you were thinking about slip away as you continue to notice the warm, tender, caring feelings.

6. Put your hands over your heart. Feel the warmth of your hands, their gentle pressure, and notice your chest rhythmically rising and falling beneath them, along with the warm tender feelings you have cultivated. These feelings and caring stance belong to you. They are now part of you.

7. Repeat these words to yourself out loud or inwardly to reinforce this kindness:

   May I be kind to myself.

   May I be present.

   May I choose caring over criticism.

   May I find peace.

8. Repeat the words three times. You may start with the words offered here and continue with three or four statements that help you activate compassion for yourself.

Bringing My Compassionate Self to Life

We have the capacity to bring a kind, compassionate presence to our lives. This is quite different from the harsh, judgmental demeanor you might be used to. In this exercise, you will develop a description of your compassionate self by filling out the following prompts.

My compassionate self is like: _____

_____

_____

_____

My compassionate self has a voice that sounds: _____

_____

_____

_____

My compassionate self says: _____

_____

_____

_____

When I connect with my compassionate self, it will help me face: _____

_____

_____

_____

Meet the Inner Critic with Compassion

Compassion is the opposite of self-criticism. In this exercise, observe your inner critic over several days, noting what triggers the self-criticism, what it is saying, what the compassionate part of you could say to the part that criticizes, and some other ways to look at the situation you are in that would be more realistic, kinder, and gentler. The trigger may be inside of you, like a thought about a situation or experience in the past, or it may be outside of you, like a situation you are in or an event that just happened.

Trigger: _____

_____

What your inner critic says: _____

_____

What your compassionate self says: _____

_____

Realistic, kinder ways to look at the situation: _____

_____

Self-Compassion Mindfulness Practice

Drs. Kristin Neff and Christopher Germer have pioneered and studied a mindfulness practice they call mindful self-compassion or self-compassion meditation. In this approach, rather than accepting your experience as it is, you aim to bring a caring presence to stillness. Instead of awareness of what is happening at the moment, your awareness is focused on what you need in the moment. Finally, you bring kindness to your suffering in the moment rather than neutral nonjudging of the suffering. For perfectionists who struggle with nonjudgment, a self-compassion practice like the one outlined here may be more easily accessible.

1. Close your eyes.

2. Take two cleansing breaths.

3. Noticing your breath, place your hand over your heart to hold and support yourself. Apply pressure to your heart as if giving it a hug.

4. As you bring your attention to the present, notice the harsh monologue of admonishment that may be coming up, the reminder to work harder, or warnings about failing. Note this is happening. Note that it is painful. This is what it feels like for someone who is a perfectionist. Allow yourself to feel that. It is a natural response.

5. Acknowledge your shared humanity. There are many others in pain the way you are. Bring to your mind all the other perfectionists who may be feeling this way. There are many others suffering.

6. Notice your breath. Stay with your breath. Notice the caring presence with you as you acknowledge the pain.

7. Bring to the moment soothing, compassionate words for yourself:

   The critic is difficult to be with.

   It is painful to acknowledge.

   I can be kind in this moment.

   May I stay caring in this moment.

   May I keep my heart open in this moment.

You Are More than What Your Critic Sees

The inner critic places a spotlight on your mistakes, your goals, how you present yourself to others, working harder, and so on. You are so much more than what your critic focuses on. You are more than what you are pursuing. Which of these are you missing out on because of your perfectionism? Use the blank spaces to write in what is unique to you.

☐ Fun and leisure activities   ☐ Going on vacation

☐ Friends and family   ☐ Trying something new

☐ Taking on a new challenge at work

☐ Being in a loving relationship

☐ Feeling happy and satisfied with life

☐ _____

☐ _____

☐ _____

☐ _____

Observing How Things Are Going and What You Have Learned So Far

It's helpful to stop to take stock of where you are on your journey of applying mindfulness to perfectionism. This doesn't mean judging where you are but checking in to see how you've been able to introduce mindfulness practice into your life. After you complete each chapter from now on, you will check in with yourself to see where you are.

We have covered a lot so far. How have you shifted how you relate to your experience?

_____

_____

Rate how well you are doing in areas of your life on a scale of 1 to 10 (1 = not at all well, 10 = very well).

☐ *Close relationships (family, friends, romantic partner)* _____

☐ *Work (school, job, career)* _____

☐ *Personally* _____

☐ *Overall (all areas combined)* _____

Key Takeaways

The ever-present inner critic became the focus of our attention. We illustrated nonjudgmental awareness as a way of countering your criticism of yourself and others around you. You learned there is a different way to relate to yourself. You were reminded that you miss out when your inner critic takes over. We introduced compassion and self-compassion practices. Developing a compassionate stance toward yourself is a different way to be than constantly evaluating yourself. Instead of striving for worth, you may direct your attention to being kind and compassionate. Here are some of the chapter's key takeaways:

→ You learned more about the content of the inner critic, its varieties of expression in your thinking, and how it feeds your perfectionism.

→ You explored ways to catch these thoughts in the moment.

→ You are so much more than your goals and the standards and achievements that you are so focused on.

→ You have a relationship with yourself, and you can cultivate that relationship to include nonjudgment, kindness, and compassion.

→ You learned a way to start tracking your evolution from the tyranny of perfectionism.

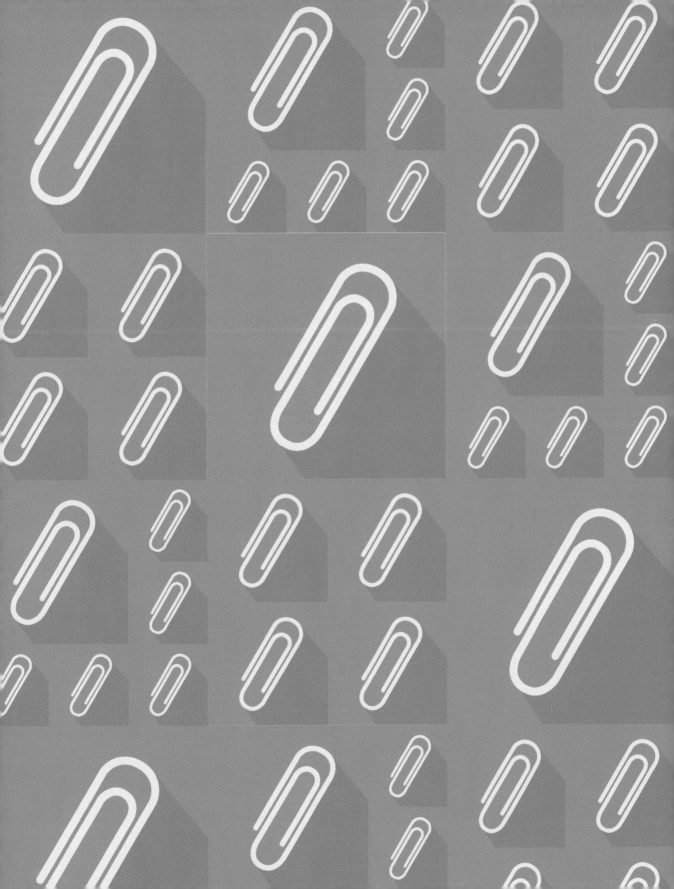

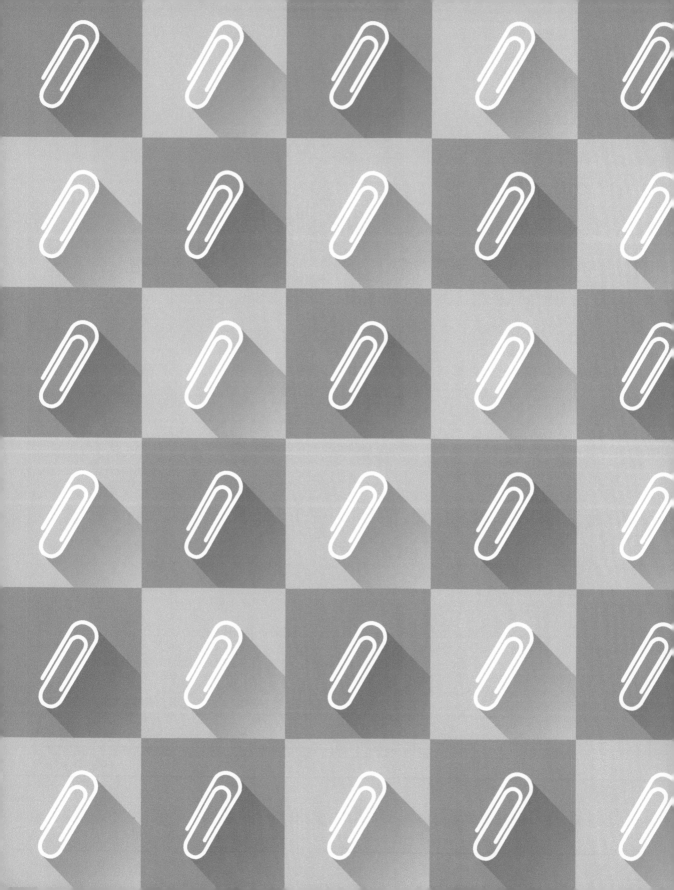

Acceptance: Acknowledging What Is, Not Clinging to What Should Be

Acceptance means seeing things as they are. You don't have to drop the standards you set, but instead use them as guideposts or lights directing your way. Imagine you are a lighthouse, always in possession of the lights directing your path. Acceptance means you can accept the present moment and whatever you are thinking or feeling. What is happening now is the only thing you know for sure. We can't control or know what will happen in the future, but we can know what is happening now. Paradoxically, this is a form of control, but a very different one than you are used to—one that fearlessly meets the present moment to see it as it is.

Some call this attitude radical acceptance, because you are meeting the present moment head-on, coexisting with whatever happens. In chapter 4, we directed the spotlight on your inner critic. In this chapter, we're directing the spotlight on feelings, since many perfectionists find it especially difficult to tolerate negative feelings. We also look more closely at how, in pursuit of your standards, you may have lost sight of other aspects of yourself that would give you satisfaction and enhance your well-being.

ANGELA LIVES WITH DISCOMFORT

Angela was the first in her family to go to college. She was excited to get a scholarship to attend a prestigious private college on the east coast of the United States. But while she was an excellent student in high school who was always at the top of her class, Angela experienced a dramatic decline in her grades the first semester in college. She began to believe that something was wrong with her. She brooded about poor grades on assignments and mistakes she had made, ruminating over what the professor thought about her. She became increasingly depressed and self-loathing, but she talked to no one about her difficulties. It was important for her to continue to preserve her image as the model student to her parents and friends back home. It was difficult for her not to see her mostly B and C grades as evidence that she wasn't smart, or her depression as evidence that she was doomed for a life of poor achievement. Initially, Angela found it difficult to practice mindfulness, and her judgment and evaluation mindset interfered with even short practices. She constantly asked for reassurance about whether she was "doing it right," and she found practicing for even a few minutes uncomfortable. So she started with very short practices of three minutes by first applying the skills to her judgment of her mindfulness practice. After she accepted the discomfort of the practice itself, it became gradually less uncomfortable. Over time, she became more able to accept the discomfort and negative feelings in her daily life.

Face Your Feelings

One of the most difficult things to learn is how to accept not only the positive feelings you experience but also the negative ones. Acknowledging the fear you feel about meeting your standard, or the shame and disappointment when your performance falls short, is just as important as the pride and happiness you feel when you perform to your satisfaction.

You may already be aware of things that trigger negative feelings, including reacting with frustration and anger to daily hassles, generally feeling stressed out about things that are on your plate, or feeling shame when you receive criticism. Living mindfully, as you are slowly practicing, requires that you face and accept all feelings.

A first step is to start a feelings journal to help you observe your emotional experience. In this journal, you will name, express, and try to understand how your feelings are related to your perfectionism. Feelings are accompanied by thoughts, behaviors, and physical sensations, and they also come with different levels of intensity.

For each day next week, become an observer of your feelings. Record the most intense feeling you experience each day, along with the associated thoughts, physical sensations, and behaviors. Be mindful of including a full range of feelings and the various ways in which you can describe how intense they are. Examples can include: angry, frustrated, fearful, anxious, disgusted, ashamed, sad, and happy.

DAY	FEELING	PHYSICAL SENSATION	THOUGHTS	BEHAVIOR
Monday				
Tuesday				
Wednesday				
Thursday				
Friday				
Saturday				
Sunday				

Stop, Watch, Accept, Be Present, Proceed (SWAPP)

Sometimes our emotions get all tangled up in a ball of frenzied doing, achieving, and producing. During those times, it becomes especially difficult to notice how we feel. Sometimes we call this being stressed, or stressed out, when it feels particularly overwhelming. Instead, we can become aware and, at any moment, swap this frenzied doing to being–that is, swapping the focus on the future with a focus on the here and now. Next time you're in this situation, try using the SWAPP technique:

S - Stop. Pause. Give space.

W - Watch. Look at what is happening inside you and outside you. How are you feeling? What are you thinking? What is happening around you? Who or what is there? How are they affecting you? How are you affecting them?

A - Accept. This is how things are now. Take in what you are watching.

P - Present. That is, be present. Be fully engaged in the moment of watching. Bring this presence to the next moment.

P - Proceed. Go about your day enriched by being more present in whatever you do.

Acknowledging What Is

Take about thirty minutes for this exercise, in which you will practice watching your experience. You'll engage the mind's ability to observe and accept what is going on now. Take time to record your experience three times over the next thirty minutes. Note your observations at the start for Time 1. Then go about doing something–anything–that needs to be done. Take your workbook with you. After fifteen minutes have passed, repeat your observations under Time 2. Resume what you were doing or go about doing something else. After another fifteen minutes have passed, repeat your observations under Time 3.

Time 1

What is happening? _____

_____

_____

What do you see? _____

_____

_____

What do you hear? _____

_____

_____

What do you feel? _____

_____

_____

Time 2

What is happening? _____

_____

_____

What do you see? _____

_____

_____

What do you hear? _____

_____

_____

What do you feel? _____

_____

_____

Time 3

What is happening? _____

_____

_____

What do you see? _____

_____

_____

What do you hear? _____

_____

_____

What do you feel? _____

_____

_____

Diaphragmatic Breathing

Also known as belly breathing or abdominal breathing, diaphragmatic breathing is a tried-and-true way to develop the foundational skill of awareness and attention to your breathing. This method is called diaphragmatic breathing because you use your diaphragm as a guide. The diaphragm sits between your lungs and your belly. When you inhale air into your lungs and your belly is in a relaxed state, your diaphragm will push your belly out. A baby's belly can be observed expanding and contracting this way. This natural state of breathing optimally is how babies begin life, because they are unburdened by the stress and tension in the world. Consciously attending to breathing in this way has many benefits.

You can practice diaphragmatic breathing in any position, but when first learning, it's best to lie down with your hands at your sides. As you inhale, your lungs expand and your belly will be pushed out. As you exhale, your lungs will deflate and your belly will contract.

Pick a time each day for the next week to practice diaphragmatic breathing. Pay attention to the air as it enters your nose and travels downward to fill your lungs. Feel the air leave your body on the exhale. As you proceed, try to breathe as slowly as you can as you fill your lungs with air. Over time, you will find that your lung capacity increases, and your inhales and exhales gradually become longer.

You Are More than What You Strive For: Creating a Realistic Self-Portrait

When you are so focused on aiming for a goal or achievement, you miss other aspects of your life that can give you joy and peace. You see or perceive yourself as existing on one or a few dimensions and evaluate yourself in these dimensions when there is more to you. We have multiple selves across time and across the places we spend our time—and these aspects of self can vary in importance. You can begin to check in with yourself to see how things are going across your life and to perhaps provide more effort in certain aspects. The domains in which adults typically describe and evaluate themselves have been studied extensively by Dr. Susan Harter and colleagues. These domains appear in the next exercise as they appear in the Self-Perception Profile for Adults.

Use the following exercise to describe yourself in each of the domains below:

Sociability: *Behavior with other people and how much you are at ease with others, like to meet new people, and are fun to be with*

_____

_____

Occupational: *How you see your competence in your major occupation, which could be your job, work, or school; how competent, productive, and proud you are*

_____

_____

Caring for Others: *Nurturing, caring, and fostering growth in others*

_____

_____

Athletic Ability: *Abilities in sports and engaging in physical activities*

_____

_____

Physical Appearance: *Physical attractiveness*

_____

_____

Adequate Provider: *Supplying the means to support yourself and others who depend on you for material needs*

_____

_____

Morality: *Living up to moral standards and ethical standards of conduct*

_____

_____

Household Management: *Handling activities in the household; being organized at household tasks, being efficient, and generally keeping your household running smoothly*

_____

_____

Intimate Relationships: *Close, meaningful interactions or relationships with your partner, lover, or special friend; seeking out close, intimate relationships and feeling free to communicate openly in a close relationship*

_____

_____

Intelligence: *The ability to learn and know; feeling smart, understanding things, and feeling intellectually capable*

_____

_____

Sense of Humor: *The ability to see the amusing side of things; the ability to laugh at oneself and the ironies of life, as well as finding it easy to joke or kid around with friends and colleagues*

_____

_____

What Is Your Authentic Self?

In the previous exercise, you described how you see yourself in various domains. What is your authentic self? Your ability to act in harmony with your true inner self can gradually become compromised from childhood to adulthood. You can distort your real inner self by seeking the approval of others and pursuing the goals and achievements you think will give you value in the world. Your inner self is pure and needs nothing else to be of value. Acceptance helps prevent the preoccupation with things you attach to your worth or value. You are worthy because of your unique humanity, not because of things you have, do, or achieve.

In the following table, indicate how important each domain is in your life now, then indicate whether you might need to shift your attention and effort in the domain to become more like your true self.

DOMAIN (DESCRIBE YOURSELF)	IMPORTANCE (0 TO 5: NOT IMPORTANT TO VERY IMPORTANT)	SHIFT (Y/N)
Sociability		
Occupational		
Caring for Others		

→

DOMAIN (DESCRIBE YOURSELF)	IMPORTANCE (0 TO 5: NOT IMPORTANT TO VERY IMPORTANT)	SHIFT (Y/N)
Athletic Ability		
Physical Appearance		
Adequate Provider		
Morality		
Household Management		
Intimate Relationships		
Intelligence		
Sense of Humor		

Describe Your Authentic Self

Perhaps you now have a glimmer of your authentic self. Work through the following prompts to help you develop a clearer picture of it.

When is the last time you experienced your authentic self? _____

_____

_____

How has your perfectionism pushed your authentic self aside? _____

_____

_____

What would your authentic self's life look like? _____

_____

_____

Accepting Difficult Emotions: RAIN

Expert meditation teachers use the acronym RAIN to describe a four-step mindfulness practice that is particularly effective for accepting difficult emotions. It was introduced initially by Michele McDonald, a vipassana meditation teacher, and has been widely taught by Dr. Tara Brach, a psychologist and meditation teacher who has also recently published a book on the practice by the same name. Initially, use this as a stand-alone practice for ten to fifteen minutes. Over time, you may use a shorter version with all the steps any time you feel an uptick in negative feelings throughout the day.

R—Recognize What's Happening

Recognize the feeling. Label and name the feeling. Notice other things that you are experiencing, such as physical sensations or thoughts. Common experiences may include a critical inner voice, feelings of shame or fear, a deep sense of unworthiness, anxiety, or depression. Note whether you have an impulse to do what you typically do to avoid these feelings. This could include excessive busyness, paralysis and procrastination, addictive behaviors, and unhealthy attachment—all maneuvers to avoid feeling shame and fear.

A—Allowing

Allowing means letting the thoughts, emotions, feelings, or sensations you have recognized simply be there. Accept that they are here, now. Continue to notice whether you have an impulse to take your attention to something else to distract yourself from what's happening, or to pretend it's not there. Stay with the experience. Know it fully, perhaps by using the neutral compassionate voice to narrate what is happening. Acknowledge the experience fully, no matter how unpleasant it feels or how difficult it is to admit.

I–Investigate

Investigating means being curious. Continue to focus on what you are experiencing. Pause. Ask: *What exactly is happening? What do I need now? What needs my attention? What am I believing? What does this feeling want from me?* Make sure you ask all these questions from the compassionate self you are beginning to know.

N–Nurture

Don't get caught up in the experience. Don't let it pull you somewhere dark where you lose yourself. Actively engage your compassionate self. Open your heart. Make a gesture of kindness to yourself, for yourself. You can gently place your hand on your heart and remind yourself that your compassionate self is always present and on call.

Reflection on Facing Feelings

Our feelings, especially uncomfortable distressing feelings, are often the most difficult parts of our experience to accept. Anxiety, fear, sadness, and shame feel bad. We don't want to feel these negative emotions, but we do. Using the following prompts, consider which feelings make you the most uncomfortable:

The most difficult feeling to experience is _____

_____

I avoid this feeling by _____

_____

_____

_____

_____

_____

Seven Small Steps toward Greater Acceptance of Painful Feelings

Accepting negative feelings is very difficult. The human tendency is to resist and avoid expressing these painful feelings. Resisting and avoiding does not make the feelings disappear. Rather, when unacknowledged, they resurface. Feelings are signals pointing to important information about your well-being. Look back at the "Face Your Feelings" exercise on page 62 and choose the two feelings that you dislike and resist most, completing the seven steps for each.

Name the feeling: _____

1. When you noticed the feeling, where were you, who were you with, and what was happening? _____

   _____

   _____

2. Feelings appear with different levels of intensity. How intense was the feeling on a scale of 1 to 10, where 1 is not very intense and 10 is the most intense you have ever felt that feeling? _____

3. How did you resist the feeling? _____

   _____

   _____

4. What thoughts about yourself appeared with the feeling? What did having that feeling in that moment say about who you are? _____

   _____

   _____

5. What did you learn from important people in your life about having this feeling?

   _____

   _____

   _____

6. Imagine yourself now in that same situation having that feeling. Close your eyes if that helps. Imagine that instead of resisting the feeling, you are your mindful self, acknowledging the feeling, feeling it, allowing it to be present with you, holding it a bit longer than you did before.

7. What would you say about yourself now regarding having that feeling? _____

_____

_____

Name the feeling: _____

1. When you noticed the feeling, where were you, who were you with, and what was happening? _____

_____

_____

2. Feelings appear with different levels of intensity. How intense was the feeling on a scale of 1 to 10, where 1 is not very intense, and 10 is the most intense you have ever felt that feeling? _____

3. How did you resist the feeling? _____

_____

_____

4. What thoughts about yourself appeared with the feeling? What did having that feeling in that moment say about who you are? _____

_____

_____

5. What did you learn from important people in your life about having this feeling?

_____

_____

_____

6. Imagine yourself now in that same situation having that feeling. Close your eyes if that helps. Imagine that instead of resisting the feeling, you are your mindful self, acknowledging the feeling, feeling it, allowing it to be present with you, holding it a bit longer than you did before.

7. What would you say about yourself now regarding having that feeling? _____

_____

_____

Observing How Things Are Going and What You Have Learned So Far

We have covered a lot so far. How have you shifted how you relate to your experience?

_____

_____

Rate how well you are doing in areas of your life on a scale of 1 to 10 (1 = not at all well, 10 = very well).

☐ *Close relationships (family, friends, romantic partner)* _____

☐ *Work (school, job, career)* _____

☐ *Personally* _____

☐ *Overall (all areas combined)* _____

Key Takeaways

Acceptance of things as they are now makes the future-oriented focus of the perfectionist almost impossible. Negative feelings are particularly difficult to sit with and express. We discussed how your striving for perfection comes at the cost of your true self. Let's reflect on the key takeaways of this chapter:

→ Acceptance is embracing all experiences occurring in the present moment.

→ Discomfort and negative feelings are particularly difficult to allow.

→ You are so much more than your goals, standards, and achievements. You began to explore yourself more completely, noticing aspects of yourself that stay suppressed and hidden because of your perfectionism.

→ Perfectionism thrives at the cost of your authentic self.

→ You practiced ways to embrace all that the present moment has to offer, including two powerful exercises conveyed in the acronyms SWAPP and RAIN.

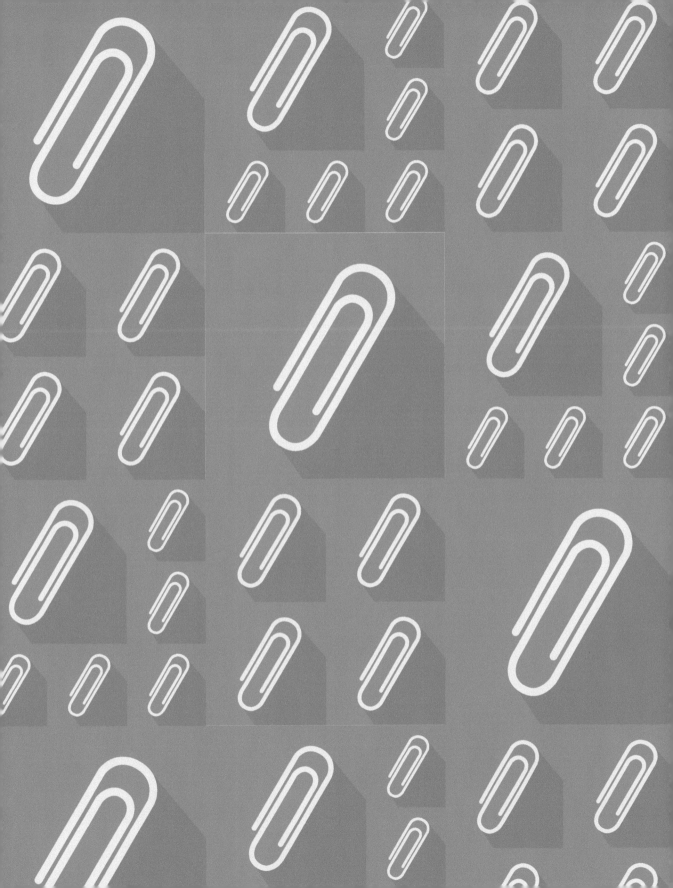

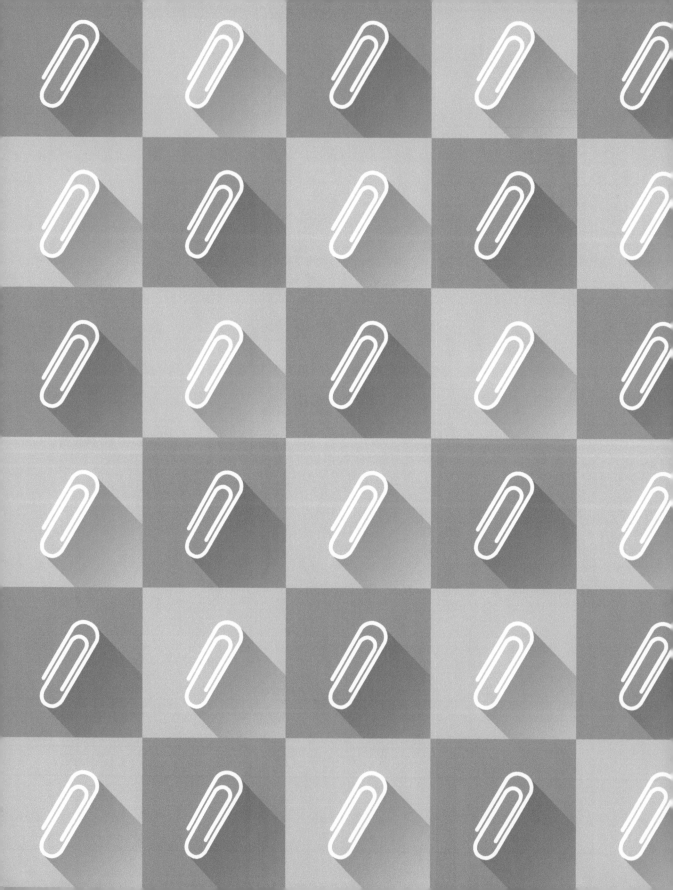

Patience: Not Rushing Yourself

I t took several decades for you to develop into the way you are now, including the parts that seem to be not working. The path to transformation therefore will also likely be long—at least longer than the discomfort wants to tolerate. It's important to remember that things will evolve in their own time with an unknown result, but this attitude is a challenging one for perfectionists, who have clear ideas about what they must achieve and when.

Mindfulness practice isn't a magical solution. Although it has the potential to have a profound impact, it is only one of the elements that can assist with addressing the ways in which your perfectionism has infiltrated your relationships, career, and recreational life. Understanding how your perfectionism took root and what currently drives it will hopefully help you become more patient with yourself and your process of change.

In this chapter, I'll provide tools to cultivate patience. A patient stance to your mindfulness practice is key. Take the time to use the practices and don't expect anything in particular to happen. We examine the roots and current drivers of your perfectionism, and include exercises to help you slow down and become more patient.

JADA—PERFECTIONISM IS MY FAMILY LEGACY

At times, Jada thought she could hear her father saying, "Straighten up. Do it again. You will never get anywhere unless you are better than all the others." An athlete who held high school and college track records, Jada was still compensating for getting injured and not making it to the Olympic team. She had a plan—marriage by age thirty, house closely following, and a promotion every two years. Jada viewed these standards in clear-cut terms, including her time frame for accomplishing them. But at thirty-five, she had attained everything except the relationship she so desired. She had a difficult time reconciling the shame she felt and the associated fear of being inadequate, along with the concern she had about how others were judging her. She often felt that her father, now deceased, would have been disappointed because she hadn't attained everything she wanted and that he expected her to. When two of her friends got married, her generalized anxiety increased, as did her hopelessness about the future.

Jada came to understand how her perfectionism was at the root of both her anxiety and her difficulty maintaining romantic relationships. She realized how her father's unwavering expectations of high academic and athletic achievement, although helpful in many ways, contributed to her drive to succeed. So she began to reevaluate her standards. As she recalled the complexity of her dad, and his saying that "nothing happens before it is time," she began to shift her perspective. She became more patient as she developed her mindfulness practice and took a steady, mindful presence to her life.

Your Theory about the Roots of Your Perfectionism

You are the expert in your own experience. With reflection and observation, you develop your inner sage—the part that holds the wisdom about you. The wise part of you can step back to reflect, embrace uncertainty, integrate information, and recognize and acknowledge the complexity of things. That is, recognize what is good and what is bad, what is certain and what is uncertain, what is positive and what is negative, what is strength and what is weakness, all without needing to reconcile in either direction. The sage knows that both sides, and all that's in between, reflect the complexity of our human experience.

What does the sage in you know about the origins of your perfectionism?

_____

_____

_____

_____

_____

Roots of Perfectionism in Early Experiences

In our early experiences in our families and other settings, we get verbal praise and other rewards by excelling. We learn about the values and goals of people we care about, and we adopt them because they are important to those people. In some families, there is clear communication of standards for achievement, athleticism, morality, and leadership. In truth, you may have internalized an infinite number of standards because adults and peers who were important to you valued these standards. In some families, there may have been a focus on criticism as a motivator for behavior. In others, there may not have been clear verbalization of perfectionistic thinking and behavior, but important adults may have demonstrated patterns in their own behavior that you emulated.

The following is a nonexhaustive list of some of the developmental origins of perfectionism. This is where a mental health professional could help you put all these pieces together, but you can also consider it yourself. Place a checkmark next to each factor that may apply to your early experience.

☐ High or specific parental expectations

☐ Experiences of criticism and judgment

☐ Harsh and controlling parents

☐ Parents overconcerned about mistakes

☐ Lack of parental involvement

- ☐ A need to cause no trouble to an overwhelmed parent
- ☐ Longing for acceptance and a need to feel connected
- ☐ Traumatic and aversive early experiences
- ☐ Parents communicating specialness
- ☐ Rewards for high achievement

- ☐ Observing family members engage in perfectionistic behaviors
- ☐ Early success as a gifted student with self-worth tied to performance
- ☐ Experiences of invalidation
- ☐ Family value on presenting a specific image to others
- ☐ Unfair expectations of others combined with experiences of rejection

Unrelenting Standards Drive Perfectionism

The excessively high standards that you set fuel myriad thoughts, feelings, and behaviors associated with your perfectionism. These high standards are stealthy contributors to your current perfectionism. They operate outside of your consciousness but nevertheless have a profound impact on your behavior. These standards, which function as measures of success, are all too often unrealistic and unachievable. Standards may be evident in your self-talk as rules like: "I should," "I must," or "If I don't." Let's bring these standards out of hiding and into consciousness, examining them across different life domains. In addition to the following categories, fill in three other domains that are specific to you, and list the standards you hold in them.

Domain	Describe Standard
Academics and School	_____
	_____
Parenting	_____
	_____
Professional Life	_____
	_____

Health and Fitness   _____

_____

Romantic Relationships   _____

_____

Social Life   _____

_____

_____   _____

_____

_____   _____

_____

_____   _____

_____

Trust Yourself to Be Patient and Less Attached to Your Standard

Now let's look at each standard and how you can allow yourself to become less attached to it. Use the following prompts as a guide:

Name a task, activity, or pursuit for which you have an unrelenting or unreasonable

standard: _____

_____

_____

Write down the outcome or result you would like to see: _____

_____

_____

As you write about this outcome, what are you feeling and thinking now?

_____

_____

_____

Let the outcome go, because it will always be uncertain. Instead of focusing on the outcome, imagine instead that you are bringing your attention and effort to everything associated with this task, activity, or pursuit in each particular moment. How are you behaving, thinking, and feeling?

_____

_____

_____

Reflecting on Impatience

Impatience is the opposite of being patient, and it involves not being able to tolerate what is happening to you now. It often occurs with daily hassles, when other people behave in ways you don't like or expect, and with yourself. Irritability, frustration, and restlessness are feelings that often occur with impatience. Your body also changes. You may clench your face, your muscles may become tense and tight, or your heart may begin to race.

Using the following prompts, think about the past two weeks. Note the times you were impatient, who or what you directed your impatience toward, how you felt, and what happened in your body. After you have reflected, imagine how you could have brought a mindful presence to these situations.

Examples of my impatience over the past two weeks: _____

_____

_____

How I could have brought a mindful presence to these situations? _____

_____

_____

Patience Observation

For perfectionists, patience is the ability to stay oriented and anchored in the present when you are anxiously anticipating perfection in the future. It means detaching from that future and remaining open to and observant of what is happening now. Acting impulsively, compulsively, and without awareness is antithetical to a patient attitude.

For this exercise, you will bring your mindful awareness to your daily life and conduct an experiment to see if you can catch yourself having an attitude of patience. Set an alarm to go off at the same time every day for the next five days. Choose a time when you are likely to have your workbook available. When the alarm goes off, respond to the following statements using a three-point scale: 1 = not at all true, 2 = a little true, 3 = very true.

☐ I am open and aware to the present moment.

☐ I am paying attention to what I am doing.

☐ In this moment, I am not distracted or having thoughts about the future.

☐ I am certain that, no matter what happens, I will deal with it.

☐ I trust that things will work out.

☐ I am rushing through without paying attention.

Drivers of Your Perfectionism

Drivers of your perfectionism include cultural and social messages, temperament, and fear of inadequacy. They are called drivers because they have a lot to do with how you came to be a perfectionist in the first place and may continue to contribute to maintaining ways of thinking, feeling, and behaving. Each of these are described in this exercise, though it isn't an exhaustive list. Consider to what degree each is relevant to you by answering the questions after each driver description.

Cultural and Social Messages

The communities and larger culture in which you grew up may have made clear what features of appearance, academic achievement, or other markers of success were valued. These messages came from the adults around us in any of the places that we spent time (home, school, religious community), or from media. Messages from media (television, movies, print) and social media and networking sites provide ongoing communication of what is valued.

What messages did you get from those around you and in the media about success, achievement, or measuring up to others?

_____

_____

What are the messages that haunt you now?

_____

_____

Rewrite the messages to incorporate the attitudes we have covered so far: beginner's mind, nonjudgment, acceptance, and patience.

_____

_____

Temperament

One of the many factors potentially related to your perfectionism is your unique makeup. Temperament, which involves how inherently sensitive you are to things in your environment and how reactive you are to things in general, can contribute.

Some of us come into the world with greater sensitivity and a tendency toward high levels of emotionality. To what extent does this describe you?

_____

_____

How does this factor contribute to your perfectionism now?

_____

_____

How can you address this factor in a mindful way?

_____

_____

Fear of Inadequacy

Self-worth that's based only on your success and achievements inevitably leads to fears that you will not live up to these standards. When you do not live up to your expectations or those of others, you interpret why this is so. Often your interpretation is that you are inadequate or defective.

To what extent does this describe you? When was the first time you became aware of your prioritizing achievement and/or living up to the expectations of others?

_____

_____

How does this factor contribute to your perfectionism now?

_____

_____

How can you address this factor in a mindful way?

_____

_____

Three-Part Breath

Bring attention to your nose, throat, and lungs. In this practice, you will breathe like a wave. Let the wave evolve in three parts. Imagine it progressing, starting way down in your pelvis and abdomen, moving up your body into the solar plexus and lower ribs, and finally ending in your chest. Initially, the belly and navel will move out from the body as the diaphragm extends. As the breath moves up your body, your belly and navel will move toward the spine. Let the exhale effortlessly wave back down from your collarbones to the pelvic floor. You may like to place one hand on your belly and the other on your chest to help guide your breath.

There is no right way to do this. Be patient in seeing how this different orientation to breath evolves. This is just another way to practice mindful breathing. If your mind wanders away from your breath and body, gently let your attention and mind come back to them.

Practice for five minutes seated or lying down.

Seated Meditation

We have now built up to you trying seated meditation. Recall that meditation cultivates mindfulness and that you can learn mindfulness through meditation. You can practice mindfulness in any place at any time–you don't need any special props. But seated meditation sometimes seems far easier than it really is; in reality this meditation requires intense focus.

1. Find a place to sit. You may sit on a chair that allows your feet to comfortably touch the floor. You may also sit cross-legged on the floor.

2. Place your palms on your thighs or anywhere they feel comfortable on your upper leg.

3. As you settle in place, straighten your spine.

4. Release any tension in your body while you relax in this sitting position.

5. Close your eyes if that's comfortable for you. If not, gently fix your eyes somewhere in front of you.

6. Be patient. Start noticing your breath. Feel the air entering your nose on the inhale, then feel it traveling through your lungs and exiting your nose on the exhale. Don't do anything with your breath–just observe it.

7. There are likely to be many thoughts and feelings coming to your mind. When they arise, simply bring your attention back to your breath.

8. After a couple of minutes, you may feel compelled to move or to stop trying altogether. Notice this impulse. Be patient. Try to stay as relaxed and still as possible while you bring your attention back to your breath.

9. Try this seated meditation for ten minutes.

Bringing Mindfulness to Your Daily Life

Our focus has been on how to stay open purposefully while being fully present to what is happening both inside and outside your body, without judging your experience. Bringing this capacity to your daily life is key. Next we explore three routine situations to which you can bring mindful awareness.

Showering

Turn on the water. First, allow the water to touch your skin. Notice the temperature and whether it is pleasing. Carefully shift the temperature of the water to a level that you like. Bring your attention to how the water feels on your skin. Watch the unique fall of the water not only on your skin but all around you. Notice what you hear as the water touches the many surfaces. Reach for the cleaning agent (soap, body wash, washcloth, shampoo) you will use. Bring your attention to the smell. Notice its texture as it moves from the container to where you need to apply it. Notice how the application of it feels wherever you put it–hair, face, torso, legs. If your mind wanders to thoughts about the day, bring your attention back by engaging your senses of sight, smell, touch, and hearing to fully experience the shower.

Walking

Find ten minutes to walk. You can walk anywhere–around the office building, in your house, on a trail, or in a park. Devote the next ten minutes or so to full engagement with your feet touching the ground, one foot forward, then the next, and so on. Notice how your feet inhabit your shoes. Notice how your feet touch the walking surface, whatever that may be. It may be a rough, uneven trail or a smooth, hard tile floor. Look at the surface. Look at your feet as they touch the surface. Bring your attention to other parts of your body walking. Notice the movement of your hips, arms, and hands. Bring attention to your torso. Notice your breath. It is probably shifting as you shift the pace at which you walk. Bring attention to your head. Feel the air touching your face as you walk. If there are thoughts or feelings that come up, perhaps even feelings of pain, notice them and move your attention back to walking. Be sure to take in your surroundings. What do you hear? What do you see? Are there smells? Notice them all and take them in as you practice being fully present walking.

Getting Dressed

Your mindful awareness of getting dressed will last the length of time it takes for you to place your clothing on your body. Practicing dressing mindfully is likely to be a challenge, as you are perhaps scheduled to go to work or the store, or do something that has the potential to capture your attention. Resist the urge to push your thinking to the future task. As thoughts come up, gently bring your attention back to the here and now. Use your hands to touch each article of clothing. Feel the different textures and take in the different colors. Place each piece of clothing, one at a time, on your body. What is the sensation of a layer on your skin? Engage your nose. Is there a hint of laundry soap present or perhaps something else? Repeat until you are completely clothed.

Observing How Things Are Going and What You Have Learned So Far

We have covered a lot so far. How have you shifted how you relate to your experience?

_____

_____

Rate how well you are doing in areas of your life on a scale of 1 to 10 (1 = not at all well, 10 = very well).

☐ *Close relationships (family, friends, romantic partner)* _____

☐ *Work (school, job, career)* _____

☐ *Personally* _____

☐ *Overall (all areas combined)* _____

Key Takeaways

Patience is openness to the here and now, to each moment, trusting that things will evolve in their own time. Having a timetable for a particular outcome is contrary to the attitude of patience. It involves not only giving up on what will happen but also giving up on when you think something must happen. In this chapter, we reviewed how complex the evolution and maintenance of your perfectionism is. We used patience to examine which factors contributed to the development of your perfectionism across time and in your current life. Other key takeaways included:

→ You clarified how your perfectionism may have evolved from early experiences.

→ You identified things contributing to your perfectionism currently in your life: unrelenting standards, fear of inadequacy, cultural and social messages, desire to be in control, and fear that you are defective or inadequate.

→ You learned seated meditation.

→ You learned three-part breath to expand your tools to attune to your breathing.

→ You learned how to bring mindfulness to your daily routines.

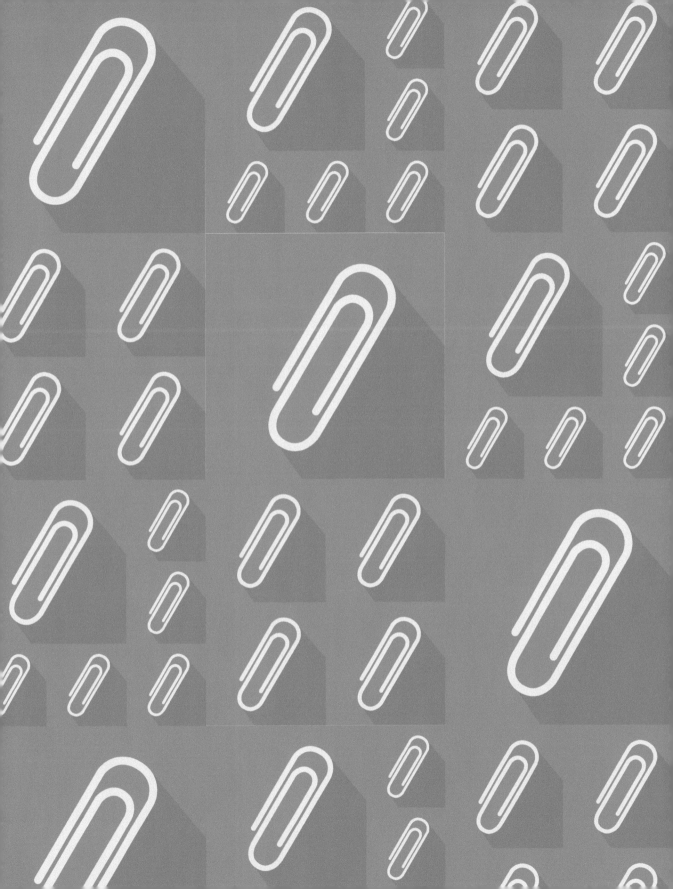

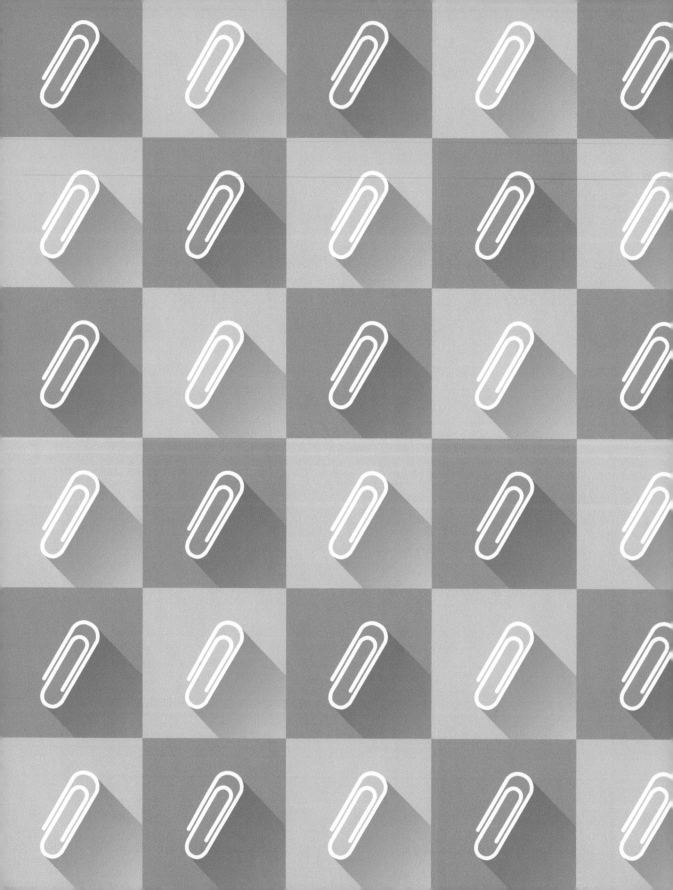

CHAPTER 7

Trust: Choosing Self-Compassion over Self-Doubt

Knowing with certainty that you will bring your best to every situation, no matter how it evolves, is key to the mindfulness pillar of trust. Worrying about your image, how you will perform, or whether you will suceed or fail makes it hard to focus on the present moment and to trust yourself. Rumination or brooding about past errors also hinders mindfulness and signals your self-doubt and deep fears of inadequacy.

Mindfulness practice helps you see that you can trust your body and breath. Ongoing practice helps you realize that there is an innate wisdom to your body, mind, emotions, and deepest self. When you trust yourself deeply, you can bring that attitude to every situation. Rumination and worry fuel self-doubt and lead you to ignore the deepest parts of yourself. The exercises in this chapter guide you to look at and respond differently to rumination and worry.

DAVID'S CYCLE OF RUMINATION

David, a college junior certain about going to medical school since he was in the tenth grade, had been binge drinking on weekends periodically since his senior year in high school. He told himself he deserved some fun since he worked so hard in school. On one hand, he was very aware of the inner turmoil and a mounting sense that life was meaningless. On the other, he was driven to pursue A grades and tied his self-worth to perfect performance. David spent most of his time studying, completing assignments, and doing additional research and projects to impress his professors. But any momentary satisfaction for getting a perfect score or A grade was overshadowed by near-constant thinking that he could do and be more. He overcommitted, never saying no to a project he felt would look good on his résumé. He constantly compared himself to peers doing more and better than he was. He would get lost in thinking about why he wasn't doing as well as others, why college didn't feel like the best years of his life as he had heard, how miserable he was, and how pointless life seemed. Occasionally, he would imagine a perfect future life, which would lift his mood slightly and allow him to avoid a boring assignment. He became aware that his life could be described in one sentence: *I study, go to the library, eat, sleep, and drink to break the monotony.* He wondered how he was ever going to achieve a balanced life.

Do You Ruminate?

The habit of mind called rumination could be represented by a hamster on a wheel, perpetually moving its tiny feet to exhaustion. The hamster goes nowhere. No problem is solved. No ground is covered. The process is mainly unproductive—unless, of course, the point was to fall in exhaustion. You might, for example, keep thinking about a mistake you made, what someone expects of you, or the thing you must do just right. These are all examples of getting trapped in the habit of thinking called rumination, which is not helpful in these situations. This habit also often occurs automatically outside your conscious awareness. Let's consider whether this habit of thinking is true for you.

Read each of the following and rate how often you think about the statement on a scale of 1 to 4, where 1 = almost never, 2 = sometimes, 3 = often, 4 = almost always.

_____ Why didn't I do better?

_____ What's wrong with me?

_____ I wish the situation had gone better.

_____ What did I do wrong?

_____ Why don't I have the friends, grades, or achievements that other people have?

_____ Why can't I get this right?

_____ Why can't I do as well as I did before?

_____ I don't fit in or belong.

_____ I am not as admired or respected as _____.

_____ I think about feeling rejected, ridiculed, or abandoned.

_____ I think about how I don't matter.

_____ I analyze how I am going to achieve something.

_____ I analyze the reasons things did not go as I planned.

_____ I wonder what people think of me.

If you indicated a 3 or 4 for more than half of these, rumination is likely to fuel your perfectionism considerably.

How Does Rumination Affect You?

How does rumination affect you? Things to consider include: Does your rumination help you get what you desire? Does it help you develop an actionable plan? Does your rumination make you feel better or worse? Do you feel energized or depleted after this type of thinking?

My rumination results in _____

_____

_____

If I were to describe my rumination as an image, I would see _____

_____

_____

When Do You Ruminate?

A variety of things can trigger your rumination. These may be stressful events, mistakes, failures, falling short of your standards, or comparing yourself with others. Triggers may be feelings, body sensations, thoughts, images, your behavior, other people's behavior, and places. Spend the next week bringing attention to your rumination by completing the following log. Describe the date and time you notice the rumination. Note the trigger and describe where you are, what you may be doing, and who you are with. Describe the content of your thinking. Describe the consequence in terms of how it affected your mood and actions. Finally, describe how the rumination stopped–did you get distracted, do something else, engage in mindfulness practice, etc.?

DATE & TIME	TRIGGER	WHAT ARE YOU THINKING ABOUT?	CONSEQUENCE?	WHAT STOPPED THE RUMINATION?

Trust Yourself to Know That There Is More to Life: Choose Flow Experiences

When you are ruminating or worrying, you are not mindfully attending to what is happening now. You are likely brooding about something that happened in the past, hyper-focused on how bad you feel, or thinking about something negative potentially happening in the future. You can proactively choose to add activities to your life that keep you so immersed that you don't ruminate or worry. This would be especially helpful for you if you are a perfectionist whose life becomes constricted and organized around the pursuit of perfection, making you neglect other things. Mihaly Csikszentmihalyi uses the word "flow" to describe those experiences in which you become absorbed and immersed in what you're doing. Flow experiences occur in those activities that engage a state of consciousness in which you are so engrossed that you lose self-consciousness and time. Instead, you feel engaged and fully connected. When the activity is over, you feel a sense of satisfaction and happiness. Flow experiences also occur when there is a balanced proportion of challenge and skill. People will often say these are the activities in which hours will go by, and they feel as if they have been doing the activity for only a few minutes. Flow experiences are an antidote to rumination, increase your experience of positive emotion, and support your engagement with your authentic self. Think about those activities in which you have experienced flow and record them here.

_____

_____

_____

Choose one of these to include in your activities over the next week. Make a plan that is realistic and not too ambitious. Choose something that you can easily incorporate into your life.

My plan is:

_____

_____

_____

What Is the Function of Your Rumination?

Everything we do has a function or a purpose, even if we are not yet aware of it. Psychologist Dr. Edward Watkins, the developer of a therapeutic approach targeting rumination, has described how the learned habit of rumination can serve different functions. Read the descriptions of some common functions of rumination in perfectionism and indicate with a checkmark which of these may be true for you.

☐ *Motivating Yourself:* You may have developed the habit of dwelling on your imperfections to help you do better. This is the belief that constantly bringing attention to your failings, in the form of that inner critic, will result in the extra effort that will make a difference. In the long run, however, you don't become more motivated and are more likely to see yourself negatively.

☐ *Understanding and Insight:* You engage in repetitive thinking to try to understand the reason something happened or to discern what something means. In doing so, you attempt to prevent falling short of your expectations and to feel more in control.

☐ *Planning and Preparing:* You run through scenarios about future events and imagine what may happen in an attempt to plan. But you don't ever do anything differently because of it. Sometimes this mode is a way to avoid actively dealing with the situation.

☐ *Avoiding an Unwanted Self:* You think about times you behaved in ways inconsistent with your ideal self to remind yourself not to become the person you fear becoming. In a way, it is as if you believe that if you do not continually spotlight these unwanted parts of yourself, you won't trust yourself to behave differently.

☐ *Escaping Tedium:* You engage in long periods of imagining your future perfect or ideal self when you are bored or want to escape a tedious or challenging task. At times, you may also replay positive performance or achievements from the past.

☐ *Avoiding the Risk of Humiliation or Failure:* When faced with a task or situation that is difficult, challenging, or where there is no certain outcome, you get stuck thinking about what might happen. This interferes with actually doing the difficult task because you procrastinate.

☐ *Anticipating Negative Criticism:* You repeatedly think about the negative criticism and behavior from others and, in doing so, attempt to minimize the negative impact because you have anticipated it. Believing you know what others' negative behavior and criticism will be might also help you feel more prepared.

☐ *Control of Feelings:* You repeatedly dwell on your negative feelings in an attempt to control them. When you start focusing on a feeling and why you feel a certain way, there is likely a cascade of emotions that lead you to a different place. For example, you feel vulnerable and start thinking about others' wrongdoing, which leads you to feel angry, which feels better than feeling vulnerable.

☐ *Making Excuses and Rationalizations:* You make excuses for your problems and difficulties. You are not doing anything about your problems, but it seems that thinking about them is better than doing nothing at all.

☐ *Gathering Evidence and Generating Justifications:* You repeatedly think about which of your standards has not been met and why things don't turn out the way you want them to.

Trust Yourself, Not the Thought: Choose Mindfulness over Worry

Worry is thinking focused on expecting something negative to happen in the future. When worry happens, we are built to react in behavior and body as if the negative prediction is actually happening. Such thoughts are chatter–they are phenomena of your mind. In developing mindful awareness, you learn to observe your thinking, especially worry. In this exercise, practice recognizing and disengaging with the worry's pessimistic prediction. List several of your worries. Next, describe how you would relate differently when these worries come up to acknowledge your trust in your ability to deal with whatever happens.

WORRY	PRESENT MOMENT–FOCUSED THOUGHT
I won't give a spectacular presentation.	I trust myself to do my best.
I am afraid I will mess up.	I prepared well; if I mess up, I will regroup.

Choose Problem-Solving: Distinguishing Unhelpful Worry and Rumination from Problem-Solving

Spending time thinking about or analyzing a problem that could be solvable is different than repetitively thinking about something that does not have a solution or is not within your power to address. It is helpful to make the distinction between when you can use your mind to solve a problem vs. when you are using your mind to ruminate in a way that is simply not constructive. Problem-solving works when you can identify a concrete problem specific to a situation for which you can take explicit steps to address in the short term. In contrast, unhelpful rumination typically involves very abstract, broad, general topics such as what happened in the past, what other people are thinking, why you are feeling bad, why you can't have or do what other people have or do, or why you don't have a certain characteristic.

Using the mnemonic acronym **SMART** can help you come up with an actionable plan. Helpful goals are **S**pecific, **M**easurable, **A**chievable, **R**ealistic, and **T**ime-limited.

Pick one of the concerns that you have identified in your log. Write down how you might address the concern stating it as a problem using a SMART goal.

Problem: _____

Specific: State a small step or specific goal regarding who, what, how, when, and

where. _____

_____

_____

Measurable: State how you will know you have accomplished the above goal. It must

be something that you or someone else can observe. _____

_____

_____

Achievable: Check to make sure the goal is attainable. It is essential to check your inclination to set goals that are too difficult. Rewrite if necessary. _____

_____

_____

Realistic: Check to ensure that you have all the resources you need (time, tools, etc.).

Rewrite if necessary. _____

_____

_____

Time-Limited: Check to ensure the goal can be accomplished within a short time

frame. For this exercise, rewrite the plan to be completed within a week. _____

_____

_____

Loving-Kindness Meditation

Loving-kindness meditation practices focus on the development of care, friendliness, and kindness by actively evoking thoughts of kindness and allowing them to develop and flourish naturally.

1. Think of someone in your life for whom you have warm and tender feelings, whether it's a child, spouse, parent, sibling, or even a pet.

2. Concentrate, focus, and bring forth those warm, loving, tender feelings to the present.

3. Hold these feelings in your heart. As you're doing that, let the child or pet or person you were thinking about slip away from your thoughts, but hold on to the feeling.

4. Take that warm, tender feeling and apply it to yourself or to others whom you might not normally feel that way about. Continue to apply that feeling to ever-larger circles of people.

Mindfulness in Daily Life: Self-Compassion Practice

Recall an interaction that made you feel bad. Bring it to mind until you feel discomfort. It is possible that it just happened, so you won't need to visualize it. Bring all the feelings and thoughts that go along with the event to mind. There is no need to try to run away from them. It happened. The distressing feelings and thoughts are here now. You can accept that they happened and they are here. First, acknowledge that you are suffering and provide yourself with a compassionate response using words that fit you. Next, continue with kind, loving words.

Say to yourself:

This is a moment of suffering.

Suffering is part of life.

Put your hands over your heart, feel the warmth of your hands, the gentle pressure of your hands, and notice your chest rhythmically rising and falling beneath your hands.

Say to yourself:

May I be kind to myself.

May I be strong.

May I protect myself.

May we learn to live together in peace.

May I find peace in my heart.

Going to Your Trusted Center

By now, you likely have encountered that hard-to-name experience when you bring your awareness to the now. For some, it feels like a plumb line or anchor, an experience of being solidly connected to yourself and your place in the world. You can trust this feeling. You can trust that this is truly you. Take the time to practice a routine activity this week in a mindful fashion. I trust that you now have the tools to breathe and then slowly take in all the aspects of what you are doing with all your senses to accept where you are without judging it or wanting to be somewhere else.

Observing How Things Are Going and What You Have Learned So Far

We have covered a lot so far. How have you shifted how you relate to your experience?

_____

_____

Rate how well you are doing in areas of your life on a scale of 1 to 10 (1 = not at all well, 10 = very well).

☐ *Close relationships (family, friends, romantic partner)* _____

☐ *Work (school, job, career)* _____

☐ *Personally* _____

☐ *Overall (all areas combined)* _____

Key Takeaways

In this chapter, we examined the habits of mind that fuel self-doubt and lead you to ignore the deepest parts of yourself. Rumination and worry are inconsistent with a here-and-now focus. Both habits of mind signal your self-doubt and deep fears of inadequacy. Whenever you engage mindfully, you see yourself, listen to yourself, and trust yourself. Rumination is punitive and critical. Worry is unpleasant. Through mindfulness practice, you begin to trust your own authority and become less reliant on others or fixed templates of what you believe you should be. In responding using compassion-focused practice you learn to nurture your true self. Keep in mind these key takeaways:

→ You came to understand rumination, what function it serves for you, and what triggers it.

→ You learned that mindful practice, problem-solving, and engaging in flow activities are antidotes to rumination.

→ You know your true self—and it isn't the person who expects you to be a certain way or who has something you desire, nor is it the rigid template you aspire to.

→ You become more of your true self with mindful practice.

→ You learned to bring mindfulness to your daily routines.

→ You learned two stand-alone practices to engage self-compassion for yourself instead of automatically engaging the critical, punitive, self-doubting stance that does not serve you.

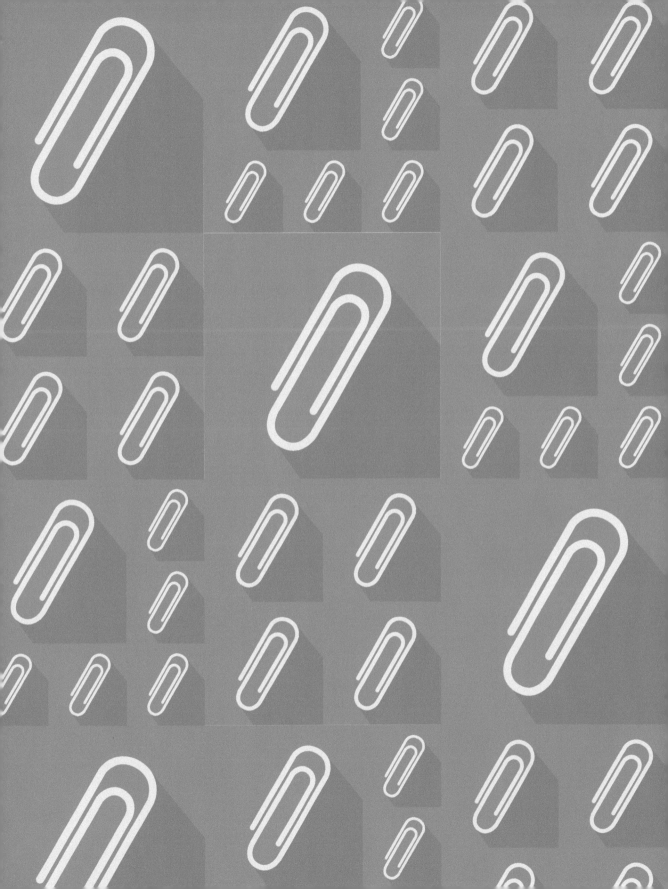

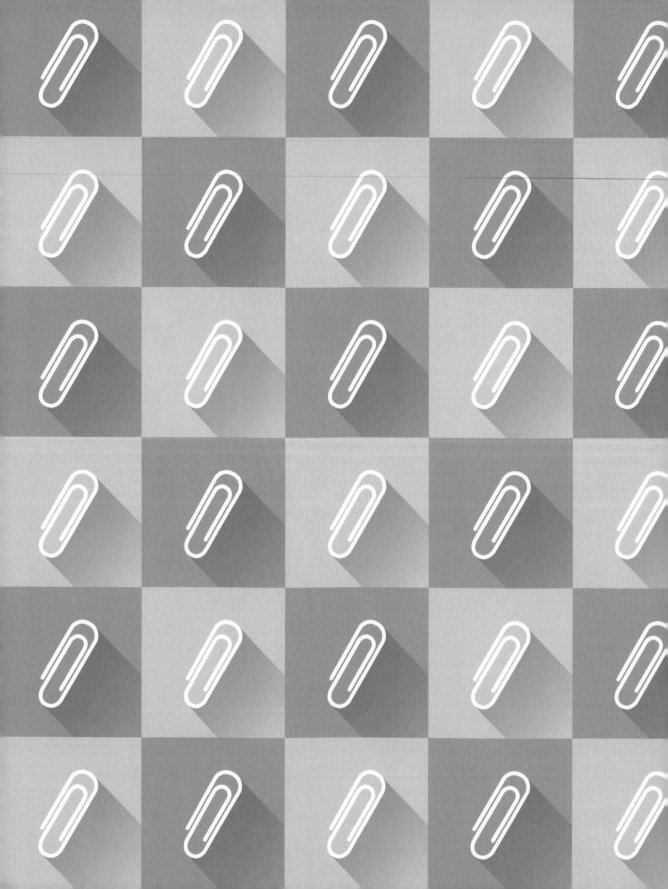

Non-Striving: Seeing Yourself as a Process, Not a Product

Non-striving, or non-doing, refers to the attitude of allowing things to be the way they are without concern for the outcome. Adopting this attitude is very difficult to do when you are so focused on a specific outcome and your self-worth is dependent on realizing this outcome. What often happens when your focus is on a perfectionist view of yourself as the product is that you miss out on other things that can increase your overall sense of well-being and happiness. You may also deny the expression of essential parts of yourself and become increasingly disconnected from others. These losses make you feel even more anxious, depressed, stressed, and generally dissatisfied.

The science of positive psychology has revealed many pragmatic ways to become more present and engaged with life. These include the cultivation of gratitude as a way of engaging with life in the present and learning the processes that will help you disengage from your focus on yourself as a product. A principle from dialectical behavior therapy (DBT) is helpful here: You are good enough the way you are, and at the same time, you can do better. Both are true. This chapter includes exercises to shift you toward yourself as a process. It also offers new mindfulness practices to try from a compassion-focused and loving-kindness framework, as these practices help increase your healthy connection to yourself and others.

KIM RE-ENGAGES

Kim is a thirty-five-year-old attorney who held high standards for herself and others. She thought that when she made partner, the steady stream of critical self-talk pushing her to work harder at all costs would stop. She also thought that she would have more time for friends, travel, reading, and all the other things that she had put on the shelf for decades. After much introspection and mindfulness practice, she finally acknowledged that she didn't get much satisfaction from the money she made and that her compulsive consumption did little for her. She realized she had made many compromises and now felt disconnected from the deepest part of herself and from her coworkers, friends, parents, and siblings. It became clear to her how contemptuous and critical of others she was. Even though she had made significant efforts to schedule time with friends and family, she felt irritated after these interactions and intolerant of their failings. Over time, she came to see how her criticism of others was related to her own ongoing cycle of self-judgment and self-doubt. Kim was impatient and critical of what she perceived as her slow understanding of mindfulness practice and the inadequacy of the tools and explanations provided to her. She said she persisted because she couldn't ignore how it had helped others she knew and felt competitive with. After finding practices that worked for her, she chose other ways to spend her time and planned activities to cultivate positive feelings.

Letter of Gratitude

When you are constantly focused on yourself and your own self-doubt, you often neglect to recognize those around you who have enriched your life. Think about someone who has been kind to you. Compose a letter to that individual describing in detail what they have done for you, how it has impacted your life, and how frequently you think of this person. Be open and transparent. You won't be sharing this letter with anyone.

_____

_____

_____

_____

_____

_____

_____

_____

Flourishing Now

Martin Seligman, esteemed psychologist and researcher, defines "flourishing" as an individual journey through good times and struggles in which a person finds meaning and purpose in things that are important to them. The core features of flourishing include the ability to experience positive emotions, engagement with life and work, meaning in life and work, positive relationships, and accomplishments. You will experience yourself as flourishing when you feel connection with others and do what you are passionate about. It is essential to realize that your flourishing is not something you have or don't have–it is a process of engaging in practices that provide the raw material together to feed the experience.

Imagine that you are living a life not without painful experiences or adversity but one that is purposeful, meaningful, and fulfilling. Think across the course of a day, a month, and a year.

Day

Where are you? _____

_____

_____

Who are you with? _____

_____

_____

What are you doing? _____

_____

_____

Month

Where are you? _____

_____

_____

Who are you with? _____

_____

_____

What are you doing? _____

_____

_____

Year

Where are you? _____

_____

_____

Who are you with? _____

_____

_____

What are you doing? _____

_____

_____

The Ten-Finger Mindful Gratitude Practice

Gratitude has been studied extensively in positive psychology, which is the scientific field devoted to how humans come to flourish and experience well-being. Simple acts of gratitude are unequivocally associated with well-being. Simply put, gratitude is being appreciative or thankful. A positive psychology researcher, Robert Emmons, notes that the full experience of gratitude incorporates two components: recognizing the good in our lives and recognizing how this good came to us by other things outside of us.

This ten-finger mindful gratitude practice can be scheduled as a more extended ten- to fifteen-minute meditation each day. You can also perform it as a shorter practice throughout the day when your inner critic arises or you become aware that you have been caught in a ruminative loop. If you are doing this as a more extended practice, find a comfortable place to sit alone with your body in a straight but relaxed posture, seated comfortably with your eyes closed. If you are doing a short version, you may subtly reach for your hands as you gaze at a fixed point in front of you.

Settle in stillness. Bring your hands to your lap. Reach for your pinkie finger on your left hand with your right hand, with one or more fingers. As you touch your pinkie, bring to mind something you are grateful for. Follow this with acknowledgment of anything that supports that thing being present now in your life. Do this for each finger on your left hand, then switch to your right hand. It may be difficult at first to come up with ten things, but keep practicing and it will get easier over time.

Deathbed Regrets: Write Your Obituary

This exercise may seem counterintuitive to a book on mindfulness encouraging here-and-now thinking, but let's do this to shift perspective. A 2018 study of hospice and palliative care nurses published in *Death Studies* indicated that expressions of regret are the second largest category of end-of-life reflections reported. First, look at the list of common deathbed regrets conveyed to hospice nurses. Then, imagine that your life will continue exactly in the direction it is taking now. Which of these regrets do you imagine might be true for you if you retained your perfectionistic patterns?

Next, write the obituary that may go with this after you die. Finally, write another obituary to reflect your shift to a fruitful and satisfying life–one in which you have used your strengths, remained attuned to living mindfully, reflected your true self, and privileged process and not product. What do you want the obituary to say?

Common Deathbed Regrets

☐ *I wish I cared less about what other people thought and lived a life true to myself.*

☐ *I wish I had not worked more than I spent time with loved ones or relaxed.*

☐ *I wish I had taken better care of myself.*

☐ *I wish I had not missed opportunities.*

☐ *I wish I had stayed in touch and spent more time with my friends.*

☐ *I wish I had pursued my dreams and taken more risks.*

My Current Life Obituary

_____

_____

_____

_____

_____

_____

_____

My Mindful Life Obituary

_____

_____

_____

_____

_____

_____

_____

_____

Hourglass Meditation or Three-Minute Breathing Space Meditation

This short meditation is a tried-and-true practice from mindfulness-based cognitive therapy that takes about three minutes and is accessible to you any time. We will use it here as an antidote to the self-attacking, self-deprecating thought loop you may find yourself in. It is called the hourglass meditation because it proceeds in three parts, each taking a minute in which you expand, narrow, and then expand your awareness again. Your cue to initiate this practice is the awareness that you have been caught in a ruminative loop.

Step 1: Bring your body to stillness. Close your eyes if that is comfortable for you. Examine what is going on in your mind. What thoughts are present? What sensations are there in your body? What feelings are here? You are not trying to change anything–you are accepting the thoughts and other sensations that are occurring. You have opened fully to what is already here.

Step 2: Let go of the contents of your mind and focus your attention exclusively on your breath. Bring your awareness to your breath as it enters your body, travels through it, and exits. If your mind wanders, gently bring it back to your breath.

Step 3: Expand your awareness, moving your attention outward. Bring attention to your whole body and all the sensations–your breath, your sitting on the chair, the sensations on the skin, how your body feels in the room. Expand your awareness to what are you sensing outside your body, connecting with the space you're in. Allow your eyes to open.

Your True Self in the Language of Values for Each Life Domain

Values are a way of describing what is most important to you. Different from goals, or things you aspire to, values are never completed. They are qualities that you embody as a person, as well as ideals that motivate you across time and situations. They are ways in which you want to be, who you want to be, and what you want your life to be about. Looking closely at your values is a common strategy in acceptance and commitment therapy (ACT). For perfectionists, values related to success and achievement are very prominent. In this exercise, think about other values that are important in each domain of your life. You can use a sentence to describe the value if a single word is not enough. The list of possible values is long, but here are some to think about: creativity, independence, innovation, perseverance, wisdom, peace, justice, helpfulness, honesty, loyalty, connection, kindness, humility, respect, courage, honor, self-discipline, security, excitement, and variety.

Domain	Values
Academics and School	Example: *I welcome the challenge of learning and growing.*

_____

_____

_____

_____

Parenting

_____

_____

_____

_____

Professional Life

_____

_____

_____

_____

Health and Fitness

_____

_____

_____

_____

Romantic Relationships

_____

_____

_____

_____

Social Life

_____

_____

_____

_____   _____

                      _____

_____   _____

                      _____

_____   _____

How Does Your Life Match Your True Self and Values?

Your focus on achievement and perfection may leave you spending most of your time, effort, and energy on only a few things that are important to you. Taking time to think about how much your life matches what you value and, therefore, how your current life expresses your true self can help you understand unhappiness and dissatisfaction in your life. In this exercise, look closely at each area of your life and rate how much you live consistently or fully with your values in each domain. A 10 indicates that you are living fully in concert with your values. A 1 means that you are not all living consistently with your values in that area of your life.

DOMAIN	LIFE MATCH TO TRUE SELF 1–2–3–4–5–6–7–8–9–10 Living Inconsistently with My Values Living Consistently with My Values
Academics and School	
Parenting	
Professional Life	

Health and Fitness	
Romantic Relationships	
Social Life	

Your Plan to Shift to a More Authentic Life Consistent with Your Values

Now that you've taken the time to look at your life, it has no doubt given you a glimpse of how you may focus on what is important to you beyond yourself and your achievements. Think of three to five areas where you would like to shift perspective and do something different. Look at the exercise in which you wrote down your important values ("Your True Self in the Language of Values for Each Life Domain" see page 116). The following questions may also help guide you to identify the shifts you can commit to:

In what ways can I demonstrate and develop my values?

In what ways can I demonstrate what I stand for?

What personal qualities can I show to others?

In what ways can I treat myself differently?

In what ways can I treat others differently?

_____

_____

→

_____

_____

_____

_____

_____

_____

Mining the Moment: Gratitude Gems

Pick a particular day for this exercise. Throughout that day, stop at the top of the hour to notice experiences and aspects of your life that you don't normally take note of but that you are grateful for. Look around to take in the pleasing elements of your surroundings. It could be a picture on the wall, a thriving plant, the rays of the sun hitting a leaf, or the delicious cup of tea you are getting ready to drink. Write these things down. Then, think about the attributes you brought to this moment–your tenacity, dependability, persistence, caring, and so on. Resist the urge to name what you don't have enough of and instead pay attention to the attributes you do have enough of. This exercise will help orient you toward gratitude. Write down at least five things every hour for ten consecutive hours. The following log starts at 8:00 a.m., but you can begin at any time.

Time   *Gratitude Gems*

8:00 a.m.   _____

                 _____

                 _____

9:00 a.m.   _____

                 _____

                 _____

10:00 a.m. _____

_____

_____

11:00 a.m. _____

_____

_____

12:00 p.m. _____

_____

_____

1:00 p.m. _____

_____

_____

2:00 p.m. _____

_____

_____

3:00 p.m. _____

_____

_____

4:00 p.m. _____

_____

_____

5:00 p.m. _____

_____

_____

Weekly Gratitude Log

Think back over the past week. Bring to mind five things that happened that you are grateful for. Remember that there are many things, both small and more significant, that we can acknowledge with gratitude. As you recall each event, write it down here:

1. _____

2. _____

3. _____

4. _____

5. _____

Loving-Kindness Meditation for Self-Love

Find a comfortable place to sit. Ground your feet on the floor. Straighten your spine and make sure your shoulders are relaxed. Release any tension in your body. Close your eyes if you are comfortable, otherwise fix your gaze a few feet in front of you. Take a few deep breaths.

Bring your awareness to your heart. Continue to rest your attention on your heart as the oxygen nourishes your body. Breathing connects you inward to all the major organs that sustain you and outward to all life you are connected to. All people share the same atmosphere, and you share with them through the breath.

Observe what is going through your mind. You may be aware of a particular stressor or problem. If you are suffering, acknowledge the suffering. This is a fundamental part of human existence. All people suffer and there are others on the planet suffering at this very moment. You are connected to them in this way.

Call to mind your good qualities. Let these qualities remind you of what is good in you. Offer the wishes of loving-kindness to yourself.

May I feel safe and protected.

May I feel happy.

May I feel healthy.

May I live with ease.

Reword the wishes in any way that resonates more for you. See yourself as a dear friend to yourself. Feel how you may feel toward a good friend. See how your face softens as you experience this tenderness and warmth toward yourself. Repeat the loving-kindness phrases.

May I feel safe and protected.

May I feel happy.

May I feel healthy.

May I live with ease.

Between each phrase, drop your awareness to your heart and body. The phrases open a door to condition your heart to become more open and accepting. At times your attention may stray from the phrases–that's normal. Just acknowledge the lapse while you bring your attention back to the phrases.

May I feel safe and protected.

May I feel happy.

May I feel healthy.

May I live with ease.

Continue for fifteen minutes. When you are ready, open your eyes. Move your body gently. Re-engage with your day.

Observing How Things Are Going and What You Have Learned So Far

We have covered a lot so far. How have you shifted how you relate to your experience?

_____

_____

Rate how well you are doing in areas of your life on a scale of 1 to 10
(1 = not at all well, 10 = very well).

☐ *Close relationships (family, friends, romantic partner)* _____

☐ *Work (school, job, career)* _____

☐ *Personally* _____

☐ *Overall (all areas combined)* _____

Key Takeaways

Not trying to get anywhere else than where you are is the essence of non-striving. What is happening in the present moment is enough. Adopting an attitude of non-striving or non-doing is impossible when you focus on achieving a particular outcome and becoming a specific product. This chapter focused on ways to re-engage with your life and values. Although the exercises may have seemed like they were asking you to perfect yourself, they were not. They offered you the opportunity to engage with your life now, not how you want to be in the future. You are good enough as an imperfect human in process. Let's look at the key takeaways of the chapter:

→ Focusing on yourself as a product often results in your losing a connection with your deepest self, relationships with others, and active participation in other life activities.

→ You learned intentional activities that help cultivate more positive feelings and behaviors, including practicing gratitude, affirming your values, and engaging in flow activities.

→ You added the practice of gratitude to your repertoire.

→ You learned how to use hourglass meditation or three-minute breathing space meditation as an everyday mindfulness practice that is accessible to you anywhere, anytime.

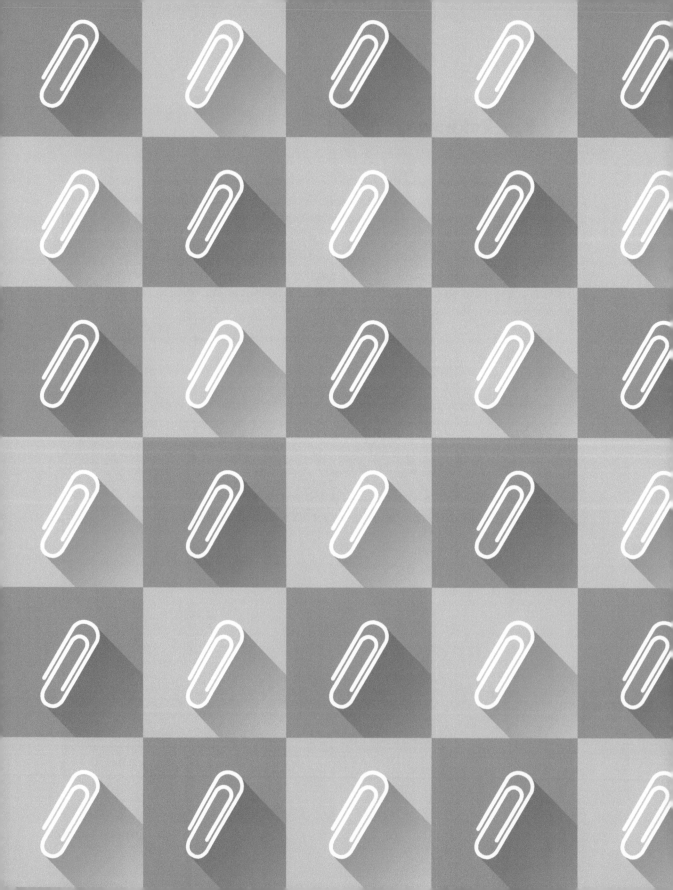

Letting Go: Making Peace with What You Can't Control

Humans aren't built for present moment awareness, to live in the moment. The ability to think toward the future, analyze, and minimize threats is one of the things that distinguishes us from other forms of life. To be human is to crave controllability and predictability. In a 2017 *New York Times* op-ed, Martin Seligman opined that we would be more appropriately named "homo prospectus, because we thrive by considering our prospects." Living in a culture that privileges mastery and control of ourselves and our environment reinforces this inborn tendency.

Desiring something can result in compulsion or fixation on that thing. Letting go is the opposite of clinging or grasping. Adopting a mindful attitude of letting go is antithetical to a fixation on wants. In the ongoing practice of letting go, it becomes apparent that the fixation is the thing that results in distress. Letting go goes hand in hand with non-striving. In this chapter, we will practice ways in which you can catch yourself clinging to something and choose a different response: to let it go. You will learn to become more attuned to the natural evolution of things, which means things won't always happen to your liking. Most important, you'll explore how to relinquish the expectation of control and engage more fully with your life now.

AJA MAKES PEACE WITH A MISTAKE

Aja welcomed the words "Amazing," "Well done," and "You're the best." She knew she had much higher standards than other people. In her family, she was trained to strive for perfect academic performance and to be intently aware of how her behavior would reflect on her family and other members of her ethnic group. Making sure that she fulfilled other people's expectations of her was second nature. She believed that making each project exceptional made her a success. But when she got a new job as an IT systems engineer, it became harder to meet these high standards. Aja began feeling constantly stressed out and overwhelmed and slept only a few hours each night as she constantly worried about doing better. Cultivating mindfulness felt alien at first. How could she approach each day free of expectations of what would happen, or how it should happen, and live with what actually happened? She began each day by slowing down. She imagined herself stepping into a new life—taking a shower for the first time, engaging her senses to feel the water, smell the soap, and feel the towel on her skin. Soon she began letting go of exactly how much she would accomplish each day. She became more able to go with the flow and use her analytical skills to adapt to whatever the day brought. She knew she had gotten the hang of it when she spilled coffee on her computer keyboard and ruined it but felt calm rather than angry at herself.

Revisiting Rumination

Rumination is a form of clinging. Mindfulness practices are very helpful as an antidote to rumination, but there are other methods to curtail this form of thinking. For the next week, record your episodes of rumination while also trying out some of the following to curb them. In the log, note how you let go of your rumination using one of the following techniques. Acknowledge that noticing your rumination is a success.

Distract: *Engage in an activity that absorbs your attention. This may be one of the "flow" experiences you identified in chapter 7 (page 99).*

STOP: *Say STOP to yourself (see page 51).*

Schedule Rumination Time: *Schedule a thirty-minute block of time when all you do is ruminate. You must ruminate for the entire time.*

Share Your Thoughts: *Contact a person you trust and share your ruminations with them.*

Journal: *Write out your ruminations in detail.*

Problem-Solve: *Write a specific, measurable, achievable, realistic, time-limited goal.*

DATE & TIME	TRIGGER	WHAT ARE YOU THINKING ABOUT?	STRATEGY TO CURB

Reflect on what your rumination is like now: _____

_____

_____

Things You Can Control and Things You Cannot Control: Choose What You Can Control

Below is a list of things you cannot control and a list of things you can control. Circle one or more items from the list of things you can control that you may start to place more emphasis on. In the following few exercises, you will explore ways to start doing things in your control that are associated with increased well-being.

THINGS YOU CANNOT CONTROL	THINGS YOU CAN CONTROL
Your thoughts and feelings	How you relate and respond to your thoughts and feelings
Physical sensations (e.g., pain, cold)	How you respond to physical sensations
Accidents	Your reactions and coping
Weather	Your preparation and reaction
What other people think or feel about you	Your behavior toward others (e.g., with kindness)
Your physique or body shape	Food and exercise to maintain health
Mistakes	Learning from mistakes
Demands others make of you	How you respond to the demands
People valuing and liking you	Actions consistent with your values
Bad things happening or adversity	How you deal with adversity

Practice Acts of Kindness: Engaging Compassion in Your Control

In your daily life, you meet and interact with many people. You may choose to engage with others by performing simple acts of kindness. It is impossible to know what impact these acts of kindness may have on the recipient. Let go of any expectation of a reward or specific result. In choosing to be kind and compassionate, you are choosing to bring a mindset of connection and caring to others.

Acts of kindness include many things: buying someone a cup of coffee, offering to do an errand, telling a clerk thank you and that you appreciate them, or performing a mundane task for a coworker. Pick a day and perform five acts of kindness on that day. The recipient may not be aware of these acts. Complete your kindness report indicating what you did. Next, make a list of the acts of kindness that you would like to do in the future that can be done within the context of your daily life. As you go forward, you may choose a "kindness day" when you include a few of these actions.

Date & Time   **Act of Kindness**

_____   _____

                          _____

_____   _____

                          _____

_____   _____

                          _____

_____   _____

                          _____

_____   _____

                          _____

Possible Acts of Kindness

_____

_____

_____

_____

_____

Visualize Your Future Self Free of the Need for Control

Imagine living a life in which you have learned how to let go and don't feel the need to control things.

How will you see yourself? _____

_____

_____

What will it feel like to be able to embody letting go and non-striving? _____

_____

_____

What will you think about yourself? _____

_____

_____

How will others behave toward you? _____

_____

_____

What role will your standards have then? _____

_____

_____

How will you relate to yourself? _____

_____

_____

Let Go of Your Unrealistic Standards

In this exercise, you will pick a specific unrealistic standard for practicing non-striving and letting go.

1. Describe the unrealistic standard.

    _____

    _____

    _____

2. Develop a realistic description that focuses on the here and now. Make sure it's focused on the process or the journey, not the outcome or destination. This is a new standard that is consistent with non-striving and letting go.

    _____

    _____

    _____

3. Describe what supports you need to follow this new standard. This may include practices, strategies, or other coping methods. Describe when you will shift to follow this new standard.

    _____

    _____

    _____

4. Try out the new standard.

5. How did this go? Describe what happened. How did you feel? Did things turn out differently than they usually do?

_____

_____

_____

6. Describe what you will do next to continue to follow the new standard.

_____

_____

_____

Shift Your Perspective to Become More Aware of Your Impact on Others

This exercise is called a Naikan Reflection, and it was developed by businessman and Buddhist priest Yoshimoto Ishin. Naikan Reflection consists of asking and responding to three questions:

What have I received from . . . ?

What have I given to . . . ?

What troubles and difficulties have I caused . . . ?

In asking these questions, you pause to examine your interactions with others from a very different point of view. You may perform this reflection by considering a particular person or relationship. It is particularly helpful if you are experiencing irritation or conflict with someone you must interact with. In such cases, you may find another way to relate to this person.

To make this exercise a daily practice, take some time at the end of the day to reflect on your interactions with others. Ask yourself, reflect, and write:

What did I receive from others today? _____

_____

_____

_____

_____

What did I give to others today? _____

_____

_____

_____

_____

What troubles and difficulties did I cause others today? _____

_____

_____

_____

_____

NAG—Notice, Accept, Let Go

This mindfulness practice can be used during your daily life. It comes from a brilliant book by Susan Pollack on mindful parenting called *Self-Compassion for Parents: Nurture Your Child by Caring for Yourself.*

Don't fight it when you notice irritation, frustration, shame, or other pesky negative emotions that are followed closely by self-judgment and critical self-talk. Notice it, acknowledge it, and then let it go. Try not to create a story about it and turn it into more than a passing—and human—moment of irritation and frustration. If it is still nagging you, practice a compassionate **NAG**.

Notice the feeling or sensation.

Allow it to linger, without fighting it off, watching it wax and wane.

Let it Go

Allowing is another way to describe acceptance. Let the thoughts, emotions, feelings, or sensations you have noticed simply exist or be there without judgment. Each thing is allowed to exist and have its own presence. This is in contrast to the impulse to pretend it doesn't exist, push it away, and withdraw from the present moment. Or to overfocus and allow it to take up all your attention and eclipse your consciousness. These thoughts and emotions are real, and you can observe them rather than let them control you. Letting go requires an active attempt to disengage your attention from the troubling experience. I find it helpful to visualize an action of letting go, such as imagining the thoughts or feelings on a balloon being lifted to the sky, or on a leaf being carried away by a stream.

Walking Meditation

In walking meditation, you move slowly and deliberately to bring your awareness to your body. You can practice walking meditation anywhere, but it's best to have a place that is private. In walking meditation, you bring your awareness to small movements as if you have all the time in the world.

1. Stand up straight.

2. Take a few mindful breaths.

3. Notice every time you move your foot forward and how it moves in the air and lands on the surface of the ground. Notice how your foot feels as it lands.

4. As you walk, pay attention to your breath.

5. Aim for a steady rhythm as you proceed slowly. Aim for one inhale and exhale per step. Inhale as you lift the heel of the foot. Exhale as you rest the foot on the surface.

Mindful Joint Rotation

This practice comes from Kristine Kaoverii Weber's Subtle Yoga. In it, you move your major joints while bringing your attention and full awareness to each joint as it moves. Bring your full attention to the joint and notice how it feels as you gently rotate it slowly at a pace that feels comfortable to you.

1. Sit comfortably in chair with a straight spine. Take three mindful breaths.

2. Begin moving your right wrist slowly, 360 degrees if you can, in a circle. Respect your range of motion and do not move past pain. Bring your full awareness to the joint and how it feels as you gently move it in a circle. Notice how it feels inside the skin and outside the skin as it moves in the air that surrounds you. Do this ten times on the right. Follow with ten times on the left.

3. Next, move your right elbow ten times. Follow with moving your left elbow ten times. As you do this, focus all your attention on the joint and the movement that it makes in the atmosphere.

4. Next, rotate both your shoulders together ten times. Again, bring all your attention to the movement and how it feels inside and outside the skin.

5. Follow with rotating your right ankle ten times, then your knee and your hip joint, each ten times. Do the same on the left side.

6. Take several mindful breaths.
   Repeat the sequence two or three times if you wish.

Observing How Things Are Going and What You Have Learned So Far

We have covered a lot. How have you shifted how you relate to your experience?

_____

_____

Rate how well you are doing in areas of your life on a scale of 1 to 10 (1 = not at all well, 10 = very well).

☐ *Close relationships (family, friends, romantic partner)* _____

☐ *Work (school, job, career)* _____

☐ *Personally* _____

☐ *Overall (all areas combined)* _____

Key Takeaways

As humans, we are inclined to believe that we can control our future and many other aspects of our lives. But there are things that we can control and things that are beyond our control. Learning the difference between what is in our power to control and what is not brings more peace and tranquility to our lives. The attitude of letting go allows us to relate to our lives in the present moment rather than focusing on a future outcome. Let's reflect on some key takeaways:

→ You identified what you can control and what you cannot.

→ You continued to shift rumination, a common form of clinging.

→ You practiced kindness, which you have control over.

→ You practiced letting go of an unrelenting standard.

→ You added walking meditation, NAG, and mindful joint rotation practices to your toolbox of mindfulness practices.

MOVING FORWARD WITH MINDFULNESS

Over the past weeks, you have taken steps to use the ancient wisdom and science of mindful practice to release the hold perfectionism has had on your life. If you incorporated one practice or made one small shift in your thinking, feeling, or behavior, you have made progress. Perhaps you have made several shifts, and you have decided to continue your use of mindfulness to enrich your life and your relationships. You may be taking only a few practices and mindfulness attitudes with you, but you can bring them to any activity or situation. Your mindfulness practice is ever evolving. It is in process, as is your development. There is no end point.

At this juncture, you may benefit from more focused training in meditation or mindfulness. Luckily, you have many options. One path is to seek training from a meditation and mindfulness teacher from any number of traditions. Another option is to seek further development of your practice through formal work with one of the many psychologists who have combined their psychological training and knowledge with that of mindfulness practice and meditation. There are many websites, books, and courses that can help further your practice.

If your perfectionism coexists with a clinically significant mental health condition or you believe that your perfectionism is part of a mental health condition, please seek the help of a mental health professional. You may do so by seeking out a type of therapy that incorporates mindfulness techniques, such as acceptance and commitment therapy (ACT) or dialectical behavior therapy (DBT). You may also seek out any of the specific mindfulness-based treatments for specific conditions. These include mindfulness-based stress reduction (MBSR) or mindfulness-based cognitive therapy (MBCT). MBSR and MBCT are time-limited group-level interventions lasting eight to ten weeks. DBT includes group and individual components, while ACT is provided individually. Each of these is described in the Resources section.

In his seminal book *Full Catastrophe Living*, Jon Kabat-Zinn states that "yoga is mindfulness." MBSR and MBCT both include yoga. For some people, the practice of yoga solidifies the practice of mindfulness. Although we did not discuss yoga in this workbook, it is worth exploring if you have an interest in it or if you resonated with the two practices that included movement—walking meditation and mindful joint rotation. My own yoga practice is essential in my toolbox of mindfulness practices. Be careful to choose a type of yoga that maintains a focus on awareness using coordinated movements of breath and body—yoga that is advertised as exercise likely is not one of these. Traditional hatha yoga, restorative yoga, lifeforce yoga, yoga nidra, Subtle Yoga, and trauma-sensitive yoga are among the options that are both accessible to everyone and solidly mindful in approach.

You may also seek out the several excellent books on practicing mindfulness, or the many apps that are available. Finally, if you have found using a workbook to be helpful, there are many other workbooks and self-help books for perfectionism—some incorporate the tools of mindfulness and some do not.

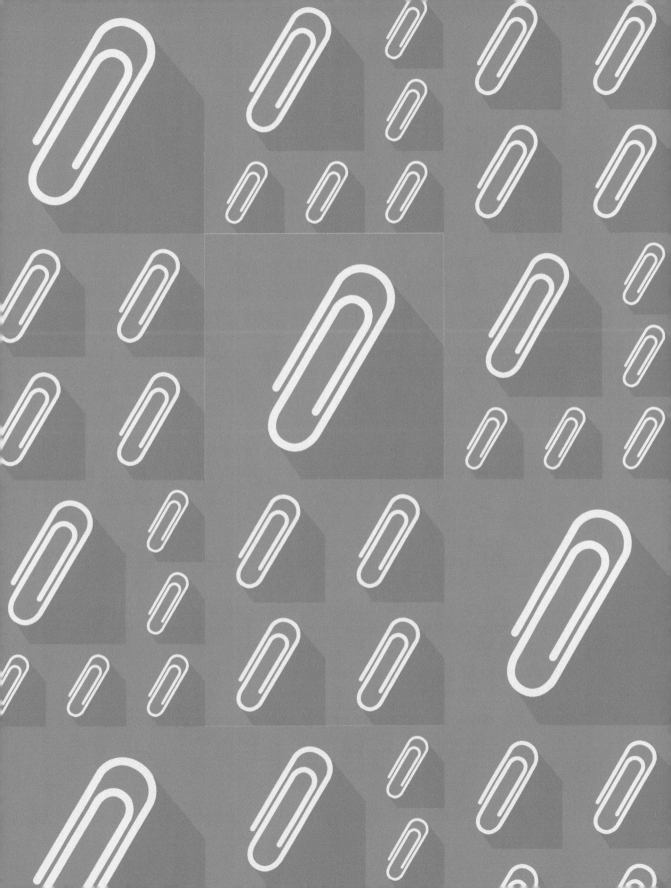

RESOURCES

BOOKS

Brach, Tara. *Radical Compassion: Learning to Love Yourself and Your World with the Practice of RAIN*. New York: Penguin Life, 2019.

Kabat-Zinn, Jon. *Meditation Is Not What You Think: Mindfulness and Why It Is So Important*. New York: Hachette, 2018.

Kabat-Zinn, Jon. *Mindfulness for Beginners: Reclaiming the Present Moment—and Your Life*. Louisville, CO: Sounds True, 2012.

Kabat-Zinn, Myla, and Jon Kabat-Zinn. *Everyday Blessings: The Inner Work of Mindful Parenting*. New York: Hyperion, 1997.

Neff, Kristin. *Fierce Self-Compassion: How Women Can Harness Kindness to Speak Up, Claim Their Power and Thrive*. New York: Harper Wave, 2021.

Neff, Kristin. *Self-Compassion: The Proven Power of Being Kind to Yourself.* London: Hodder & Stoughton, 2013.

WORKBOOKS

Kemp, Jennifer. *The ACT Workbook for Perfectionism: Build Your Best (Imperfect) Life Using Powerful Acceptance and Commitment Therapy and Self-Compassion Skills.* Oakland, CA: New Harbinger Publications, 2021.

Martin, Sharon. *CBT Workbook for Perfectionism: Evidence-Based Skills to Help You Let Go of Self-Criticism, Build Self-Esteem, and Find Balance*. Oakland, CA: New Harbinger Publications, 2019.

Ona, Patricia Zurita. *Acceptance and Commitment Skills for Perfectionism and High-Achieving Behaviors*. New York: Routledge, 2022.

Shafran, Roz, Sarah Egan, and Tracey Wade. *Overcoming Perfectionism: A Self-Help Guide Using Cognitive Behavioral Techniques*. London: Robinson, 2010.

WEBSITES

The Mindfulness Center at the University of Pennsylvania School of Medicine provides a number of online and other programs for training in mindfulness.
pennmedicine.org/for-patients-and-visitors/find-a-program-or-service/mindfulness

The MBCT website describes training opportunities, a directory of international providers, and other resources.
mbct.com

Many opportunities for training in MBSR are included for the public at the UMass Memorial Health Center for Mindfulness where Jon Kabat-Zinn developed MBSR.
ummhealth.org/center-mindfulness

Dr. Kristin Neff and Dr. Christopher Germer's Mindful Self-Compassion program combines the skills of mindfulness and self-compassion.
self-compassion.org/the-program

Mindful magazine is a monthly print and digital publication that provides accessible descriptions of mindfulness practices. They also have an article on how to find a meditation teacher (referenced in the "Finding a Mindfulness Coach" section on page 144) and recently started a service to link you with a mindfulness coach to provide individual coaching.
mindful.org

Angel Kyodo Williams is an ordained Zen master who provides many resources and opportunities to join in community practice.
angelkyodowilliams.com

Dr. Tara Brach is a psychologist, insight (vipassana) meditation teacher, and author. Her RAIN practice is one that I offer others repeatedly and is discussed in this workbook. Dr. Brach's website is filled with many guided meditations that she provides for free.
tarabrach.com

APPS

There are now many choices for apps that provide guided mindfulness practices. If you benefit from hearing the voice of someone leading you through a practice, one of these may be helpful. They all have versions that are no cost and versions with enhancements that require a subscription.

headspace.com

calm.com

breethe.com/about

liberatemeditation.com

FINDING A THERAPIST

Options for finding a therapist include the American Psychology Association locator site.
locator.apa.org

Psychologists who use evidence-based mindfulness treatments, such as MBCT and DBT, are listed on the Association of Cognitive and Behavioral Therapies website's ABCT directory.
services.abct.org/i4a/memberDirectory/index.cfm?directory_id=3&pageID=3282

Therapists who practice ACT are listed on the Association for Contextual Behavioral Science website.
contextualscience.org/tips_for_seeking_therapist

FINDING A MINDFULNESS COACH

Mindful magazine published an article on finding a mindfulness meditation teacher near you:

mindful.org/how-to-find-a-mindfulness-meditation-teacher-near-you

YOGA

Trauma Sensitive Yoga
traumasensitiveyoga.com

iRest Yoga
irest.org

Subtle Yoga
subtleyoga.com

Lifeforce Yoga
amyweintraub.com/lifeforce-yoga

REFERENCES

Brach, Tara. *Radical Compassion: Learning to Love Yourself and Your World With the Practice of RAIN*. New York: Penguin Life, 2019.

Brown, Kirk Warren, Richard M. Ryan, and J. David Creswell. "Mindfulness: Theoretical Foundations and Evidence for its Salutary Effects." *Psychological Inquiry* 18, no. 4 (December 2007): 211-37. doi:10.1080/10478400701598298.

Cheli, Simone, Veronica Cavalletti, Gordon L. Flett, and Paul L. Hewitt. "Mindful Compassion for Perfectionism in Personality Disorders: A Pilot Acceptability and Feasibility Study." *Bollettino di Psicologia Applicata* [*Applied Psychology Bulletin*] 68, no. 287 (January-April 2020): 55-65. doi:10.26387/bpa.287.5.

Creswell, J. David. "Mindfulness Interventions." *Annual Review of Psychology* 68, no. 1 (January 2017): 491-516. doi:10.1146/annurev-psych-042716-051139.

Curran, Thomas, and Andrew P. Hill. 2019. "Perfectionism Is Increasing Over Time: A Meta-Analysis of Birth Cohort Differences From 1989 to 2016." *Psychological Bulletin* 145, no. 4 (November 2019): 410-29. doi:10.1037/bul0000138.

Dimidjian, Sona, and Zindel V. Segal. "Prospects for a Clinical Science of Mindfulness-Based Intervention." *American Psychologist* 70, no. 7 (October 2015): 593-620. doi:10.1037/a0039589.

Eisendrath, Stuart J., Erin Gillung, Kevin L. Delucchi, Zindel V. Segal, J. Craig Nelson, L. Alison McInnes, Daniel H. Mathalon, and Mitchell D. Feldman. "A Randomized Controlled Trial of Mindfulness-Based Cognitive Therapy for Treatment-Resistant Depression." *Psychotherapy and Psychosomatics* 85, no. 2 (2016): 99-110. doi:10.1159/000442260.

Emmons, Robert. "Why Gratitude Is Good." *Greater Good Magazine*. November 16, 2010. greatergood.berkeley.edu/article/item/why_gratitude_is_good.

Ent, Michael R., and Mary A. Gergis. "The Most Common End-of-Life Reflections: A Survey of Hospice and Palliative Nurses." *Death Studies* 44, no. 4 (December 2018): 256-60. doi:10.1080/07481187.2018.1539053.

Flett, Gordon L., Paul L. Hewitt, Kirk R. Blankstein, and Lisa Gray. "Psychological Distress and the Frequency of Perfectionistic Thinking." *Journal of Personality and Social Psychology* 75, no. 5 (1998): 1363-81. doi:10.1037/0022-3514.75.5.1363.

Flett, Gordon L., Paul L. Hewitt, Taryn Nepon, and Avi Besser. "Perfectionism Cognition Theory: The Cognitive Side of Perfectionism." In J. Stoeber (Ed.), *The Psychology of Perfectionism: Theory, Research, Applications* (pp. 89-110). London: Routledge, 2018.

Fredrickson, Barbara. *Love 2.0: Creating Happiness and Health in Moments of Connection*. New York: Plume, 2014.

Hewitt, Paul L., and Gordon L. Flett. "Perfectionism in the Self and Social Contexts: Conceptualization, Assessment, and Association with Psychopathology." *Journal of Personality and Social Psychology* 68, no. 3 (1991): 456-70. doi:10.1037/0022-3514.60.3.456.

Hewitt, Paul L., Gordon L. Flett, and Samuel F. Mikail. *Perfectionism: A Relational Approach to Conceptualization, Assessment, and Treatment*. New York: Guilford Press, 2017.

Hill, Andrew P., and Thomas Curran. "Multidimensional Perfectionism and Burnout: A Meta-Analysis." *Personality and Social Psychology Review* 20, no. 3 (August 2016): 269-88. doi:10.1177/1088868315596286.

Hölzel, Britta K., Sara Lazar, Tim Gard, Zev Schuman-Olivier, David R. Vago, and Ulrich Ott. "How Does Mindfulness Meditation Work? Proposing Mechanisms of Action from a Conceptual and Neural Perspective." *Perspectives on Psychological Science* 6, no. 6 (November 2011): 537-59. doi:10.1177/1745691611419671.

Jha, Amishi P., Jason Krompinger, and Michael J. Baime. "Mindfulness Training Modifies Subsystems of Attention." *Cognitive, Affective, & Behavioral Neuroscience* 7, no. 2 (June 2007): 109-19. doi:10.3758/CABN.7.2.109.

Kabat-Zinn, Jon. *Full Catastrophe Living: Using the Wisdom of Your Body and Mind to Face Stress, Pain, and Illness*. 2nd ed. New York: Bantam Books, 2013.

Kabat-Zinn, Jon. "Mindfulness-Based Interventions in Context: Past, Present, and Future." *Clinical Psychology: Science and Practice* 10, no. 2 (June 2003) 144-56. doi:10.1093/clipsy.bpg016.

Koerton, Hannah R., Tanya S. Watford, Eric F. Dubow, and William H. O'Brien. "Cardiovascular Effects of Brief Mindfulness Meditation Among Perfectionists Experiencing Failure." *Psychophysiology* 57, no. 4 (February 2020): e13517. doi:10.1111/psyp.13517.

Lyubomirsky, Sonja, and Kristin Layous. "How Do Simple Positive Activities Increase Well-Being?" *Current Directions in Psychological Science* 22, no. 1 (February 2013): 57-62. doi:10.1177/0963721412469809.

Matos, Marcela, and Stanley R. Steindl. "'You Are Already All You Need to Be': A Case Illustration of Compassion-Focused Therapy for Shame and Perfectionism." *Journal of Clinical Psychology* 76, no. 11 (September 2020): 2079-96. doi:10.1002 /jclp.23055.

Messer, Bonnie, and Susan Harter. *The Self-Perception Profile for Adults: Manual and Questionnaires: 2012 Revision of 1986 Manual.* Denver, CO: University of Denver Arts, Humanities & Social Sciences, Department of Psychology, 2012.

Neff, Kristin. *Self-Compassion: The Proven Power of Being Kind to Yourself.* New York: William Morrow, 2011.

Ong, Clarissa W., Eric B. Lee, Jennifer Krafft, Carina L. Terry, Tyson S. Barrett, Michael E. Levin, and Michael P. Twohig. "A Randomized Controlled Trial of Acceptance and Commitment Therapy for Clinical Perfectionism." *Journal of Obsessive-Compulsive and Related Disorders* 22 (July 2019): 100444. doi:10.1016/j.jocrd.2019.100444.

Ong, Clarissa W., Jennifer L. Barney, Tyson S. Barrett, Eric B. Lee, Michael E. Levin, and Michael P. Twohig. "The Role of Psychological Inflexibility and Self-Compassion in Acceptance and Commitment Therapy for Clinical Perfectionism." *Journal of Contextual Behavioral Science* 13, no. 1 (June 2019): 7-16. doi:10.1016 /j.jcbs.2019.06.005.

Pollack, Susan. *Self-Compassion for Parents: Nurture Your Child by Caring for Yourself.* New York: Guilford Press, 2019.

Salzberg, Sharon. *Loving-Kindness: The Revolutionary Art of Happiness.* Boston: Shambhala Publications, 1995.

Segal, Zindel V., J. Mark G. Williams, and John D. Teasdale. *Mindfulness-Based Cognitive Therapy for Depression.* New York: Guilford Press, 2013.

Seligman, Martin, and John Tierney. "We Aren't Built to Live in the Moment." *New York Times.* May 19, 2017. nytimes.com/2017/05/19/opinion/sunday/why-the -future-is-always-on-your-mind.html.

Stoeber, Joachim. *The Psychology of Perfectionism: Theory, Research, Applications.* Oxfordshire, UK: Routledge, 2017.

Tang, Yi-Yuan, Britta K. Hölzel, and Michael I. Posner. "The Neuroscience of Mindfulness Meditation." *Nature Reviews Neuroscience* 16, no. 4 (April 2015): 213-25. doi:10.1038/nrn3916.

ToDo Institute. "How to Practice Naikan Reflection." Accessed April 28, 2022. todoinstitute.com/naikan3.html.

Watkins, Edward R. *Rumination-Focused Cognitive-Behavioral Therapy for Depression.* New York: Guilford Press: 2016.

INDEX

A

Acceptance
  about, 21, 61, 76
  of authentic self, 69-70
  case study, 62
  diaphragmatic breathing, 66-67
  of feelings, 62-63, 72-74
  of multiples selves, 67-68
  observing your experiences, 64-66
  RAIN practice, 71-72
  SWAPP technique, 64
Acceptance and commitment
    therapy (ACT), 20, 116, 139
Achievement, 12-13
Anxiety, 8
Authenticity, 119
Automatic perfectionistic
    thoughts, 40-41

B

Beginner's mind
  about, 20-21, 33, 45
  body scan meditation, 39-40
  case study, 34
  change matrix, 44
  and domains of perfectionism, 37-38
  and forms of perfectionism, 35-37
  hand-on-heart practice, 41
  and imperfection, 42-43
  mindful breathing, 34-35
  perfectionism's double-edged
      sword, 35
  and perfectionistic automatic
      thoughts, 40-41
  Perfectionistic Self-Presentation
      Scale, 38-39
  self-defeating behaviors, 42
Behaviors, self-defeating, 42
Besser, Avi, 48
Body scan meditation, 39-40
Brach, Tara, 71
Breathing mindfully, 34-35
  diaphragmatic breathing, 66-67
  three-part breath, 88

C

Case studies
  Aja, 128
  Angela, 62
  Dan, 48
  David, 96
  Jada, 80
  Jaden, 18
  Kim, 110
  Tai, 4
  Van, 34
Change matrix, 44
Compassion, 54-55, 131
Compassion seated meditation, 53
Comprehensive Model of Perfectionistic
    Behavior (CMPB), 9
Control, desire for, 8, 130, 132-133
Csikszentmihalyi, Mihaly, 99
Cultural expectations, 8, 85-86

D

Deathbed regrets, 114-115
Dialectical behavior therapy
    (DBT), 20, 109, 140
Diaphragmatic breathing, 66-67
Dressing mindfully, 90

E

Emmons, Robert, 113
Expectations, 7-8

F

Failure, fear of, 11
Fears, 11, 87
Feelings and emotions
    acceptance of, 62-63, 72
    acceptance of painful, 72-74
    RAIN practice, 71-72
    SWAPP technique, 64
Flett, Gordon, 9, 48
Flourishing, 111-113
Flow experiences, 99
Full Catastrophe Living (Kabat-Zinn), 140

G

Generosity, 23
Germer, Christopher, 55
Gratitude, 23, 110-111, 113-114, 120-122

H

Habits, changing, 14
Hand-on-heart practice, 41
Harter, Susan, 67

H

Hayes, Steven, 20
Health and fitness, 13
Hewitt, Paul, 9, 48
Hourglass meditation, 115-116

I

Impatience, 84
Imperfection, 28, 42-43
Inadequacy, feelings of, 8, 87
Inner critic, 48-52, 55, 56-57

J

Joint rotation practice, 136-137

K

Kabat-Zinn, Jon, 18-20, 140
Kindness, acts of, 131-132
Kintsugi, 42

L

Letting go
    about, 22, 127, 138
    acts of kindness, 131-132
    case study, 128
    of control, 130, 132-133
    mindful joint rotation, 136-137
    NAG practice, 135-136
    Naikan Reflection, 134-135
    of rumination, 128-129
    of unrealistic standards, 133-134
    walking meditation, 136
Linehan, Marsha, 20
Loving-kindness meditation, 104, 122-123

M

McDonald, Michele, 71
Meditation
  as an aspect of mindfulness, 24
  body scan, 39-40
  compassion seated, 53
  hand-on-heart practice, 41
  hourglass, 115-116
  loving-kindness, 104, 122-123
  seated, 88-89
  walking, 136
Mikail, Samuel, 9
Mindfulness. *See also* Acceptance;
    Beginner's mind; Letting go;
    Nonjudgment; Non-striving;
    Patience; Trust
  about, 17-20, 29
  benefits of, 26
  core mental processes, 25
  as evidence-based, 25-26
  generosity, 23
  gratitude, 23
  misunderstandings about, 24
  for perfectionism, 28, 139-140
  pillars of, 20-22
  practicing, 27
Mindfulness-based cognitive therapy
    (MBCT), 20, 26, 140
Mindfulness-based stress reduction
    (MBSR), 18, 20, 140

N

NAG practice, 135-136
Naikan Reflection, 134-135
Neff, Kristin, 55

Nepon, Taryn, 48
Nonjudgment
  about, 21, 47, 58
  case study, 48
  compassion, 54-55
  compassion seated meditation, 53
  and the inner critic, 48-52, 55, 56-57
  self-compassion, 55-56
  shame, 52
  STOP practice, 51
Non-striving
  about, 22, 109, 125
  case study, 110
  flourishing, 111-113
  gratitude, 110-111, 113-114, 120-122
  hourglass meditation, 115-116
  loving-kindness meditation, 122-123
  obituary exercise, 114-115
  values, 116-120

O

Obituary exercise, 114-115
Other-oriented perfectionism, 9, 36

P

Parental expectations, 7
Parenting, 12
Patience
  about, 21, 79, 92
  and attachment to standards, 82-84
  case study, 80
  and drivers of perfectionism, 85-87
  impatience, noticing, 84
  mindfulness in daily life activities, 89-90
  observing, 85
  and roots of perfectionism, 80-82

Patience (*continued*)
  seated meditation, 88-89
  three-part breath, 88
Perfectionism
  about, 4-5, 15
  characteristics of, 10-11
  domains of, 12-14, 37-38
  drivers of, 85-87
  mindfulness for. *See* Mindfulness
  vs. pursuit of excellence, 6
  roots of, 7-8
  types of, 8-9, 35-37
  use of term, 3
Perfectionism Cognition Theory, 48
Perfectionistic Self-Presentation
    Scale, 38-39
Perspective shifting, 134-135
Pollack, Susan, 135
Problem solving, 102-103
Professional life, 12-13
Public image, 14, 38-39
Pursuit of excellence, 6

R

RAIN practice, 71-72
Romantic relationships, 13
Rumination, 11, 96-98, 100-101, 128-129

S

School life, 12
Self
  authentic, 69-70
  as multi-dimensional, 67-68
Self-compassion, 55-56, 104-105

Self-Compassion for Parents
    (Pollack), 135
Self-criticism, 10
Self-love, 122-123
Self-oriented perfectionism, 9, 36
Self-presentation, 38-39
Self-worth, 11
Seligman, Martin, 111, 127
Shame, 52
Showering mindfully, 89
SMART goals, 102-103
Social life, 13-14
Socially prescribed perfectionism, 9, 37
Societal expectations, 8, 85-86
Standards
  attachment to, 82-84
  unrealistic, 133-134
  unreasonable, 10
STOP practice, 51
Subtle Yoga, 136-137
SWAPP technique, 64

T

Temperament, 86-87
Thoughts, automatic perfectionistic,
    40-41
Trust
  about, 22, 95, 106
  case study, 96
  flow experiences, 99
  problem solving, 102-103
  and rumination, 96-98, 100-101
  self-compassion practice, 104-105
  trusted center, 105
  and worry, 101-102

U

Unlovability, feelings of, 8

V

Values, 116-120

W

Walking meditation, 136
Walking mindfully, 90

Watkins, Edward, 100
Weber, Kristine Kaoverii, 136
Worry, 11, 101-102

Y

Yoga, 140

Acknowledgments

With deep gratitude and humility, I acknowledge all the researchers, psychologists, therapists, and mindfulness and meditation teachers whose work has informed this application of mindfulness practice to perfectionism. The clients who have placed their trust in me–and the professional practice of psychology–to alleviate their pain and suffering deserve particular recognition for their courage, vision, and willingness to change.

About the Author

Elaine A. Thomas, PsyD, is a licensed psychologist with a practice in Marietta, Georgia. She has provided mental health treatment to adults, children, and families in several settings. In her practice, she relies on multiple methods, including those demonstrated effective by research. A mindfulness practice, primarily through yoga, is an essential ingredient to her own well-being and flourishing for the past fifteen years. She has taught clinical psychology doctoral students as core faculty in two doctoral programs.